Women of Nepal
March Forward

(Travel Report)

Gabriele and Thomas Beisenkamp

Jana Shikshya Griha
Kathmandu, Nepal
2007

Publisher
Jana Shikshya Griha
(People's Educational House)
Kathmandu, Nepal
Mobile : 00977-9841351482
Emali : paudeldurga28@yahoo.com
Post Box No. : 10322, GPO, Kathmandu

First English Edition
Oct. 2007

Price
Hard cover : N.C. **600.00**, I.C. **400.00**
Paper back : N.C. **225.00**, I.C. **150.00**
Euro   : **16.00**

Press
Paru Ofiset Press
Kathmandu

From the Publisher

We are pleared much to publish the English version of the book, Nepals Frauen im Aufbruch, written in German by Gabriele and Thomas Beisenkamp in 2002 and published in Germany. In Invitation of All Nepal Women's Association (ANWA) both of them had come to Nepal to participate in the All Nepal Women's National Campaign (ANWNC) organized by ANWA in 2002. The Campaign was conducted in a most difficult condition when the king had taken all power in his hands, had imposed Emergency, all fundamental rights were banned and country-wide arrest political leaders or workers was done.

So, it was a risky thing to travel in Nepal or to participate in any countrywide public programme such as ANWAC. We are really thankful to the couple, Gabi and Thomos, for they dared to come to Nepal and participate in our national programme in such a difficult condition and that was a true symbol of international fraternity. Besides it, we are thankful to them for the book they have written giving a detailed report not only of the Campaign, but also the women's liberation movement and socio-economic conditions of Nepal. More than that, the important aspect of the book is that it is based on the first hand information, interaction and direct contact with the people of remote parts of country and rural areas. And that makes the book more authentic.

The English version of the book is published under the title, Women of Nepal March Forward. We are not sure if it tallies with the German title of the book, especially with the last words of the title, "im Aufbruch". But considering upon the nature of the Campaign, which itself was a march for rights and liberation of women, we think, the title of the English version is in accordance with the sprit of the Campaign and of the original title of the book, too. We have added a few appendixcs in English translation to make more explicit the subjects, mentioned in the book such as fraternal relation between the women of Nepal and Germany, the liberation movement of Nepal, the role of the ANWA on it and the Campaign itself. Additonally, we have given some explanatory foot notes also.

We are sorry that we could not publish all of the colour photographs given in the German edition of the book. At the same time we have re-arranged the order of all photographs and have added two more : that of an old Dalit (untouchable) iron-smith, Kul Bahadur, whom Gabi and Thomos had met and have referred in the book (Page-72) and one that of a folk dance conducted during Campaign at Okharkot (Pyuthan). The photographs of Kul Bahadur is taken by us while other one was chosen from the slides which the authors of the book were kind enough to send us. We also beg pardon that we have replaced the photograph of the cover of the German edition taking another one entitted, "Nepal's Future" from the book itself. The photograph of the cover of the German edition is kept inside (Page-7). The future of Nepal depends upon, the children. But what is required is that they should be awakened to be able enough to achieve that great goal and, this responsibility is ours. So, we are convinced, the photo choosen for the cover represents the socio-economic condition of Nepal, movement of people for change and, simultaneously, resembles the sprit of the book, which ends with the following poem :

"The children of the world fighting to survive.
But in their little hands is power for a better life."

Yes, the future not only of Nepal, but also of the whole world depends upon the "Litle Hands" wich have wonderful "Power for better life".

In spite of the fact that the book contains so much important report on the liberation movement of women, the Campaign and society of Nepal non-German speaking people of Nepal or outside had no accessibility to the information that the book included. Now, we think, the publication of the English version of the book will be of much help for those interested in the women's liberation movement of Nepal and it is with this wish and hope that we have endeavored to publish this book. If this book served this objective even a little, it would be a matter of great pleasure for us.

Durga Paudel

October 10, 2007

Contents

Confidence upon victory and future

Terai family hut.

Women from a Tharu village.

Foreword

Most readers will know Nepal as the country with the world's highest mountains. The name Mount Everest Shagarmatha or Tschomolunga, as the Nepalese call the highest mountain in the world, is enough to make the hearts of many mountaineers beat faster. More and more people from all over the world visit Nepal to go trekking through the really beautiful mountains and to enjoy the wonders of nature.

Many people also know that Nepal is one of the poorest countries in the world; almost half its population live below the so-called subsistence level, a country economically dependent on India, the U.S.A. and also Germany with antiquated production methods which does not have the chance of independent economic development.

Anyone living in Germany or the U.S.A. can often not even imagine how, not just in Nepal but all over the world, the majority of people are forced to live; what it means when over half the population live below subsistence level, when electricity supply, water supply and road connections are not something normal. In Nepal the vast majority of people have to live under these conditions. And this is happening in the age of computers and gene technology, in a time when technical possibilities have become so sophisticated that everybody could have a high level of culture.

What is largely unknown is that among the population in Nepal there is an uncompromising will for a life without exploitation and oppression. And who has ever heard of the strong and fighting women's movement in Nepal?

In an uprising against the autocracy of the king in 1990 the population fought for and gained a democratic multi-party system. It is allegedly a constitutional monarchy in which the king has usurped essential state powers. Apart from the Congress Party it was mainly a large number of democratic and Marxist-Leninist parties and courageous women's organisations that were involved in the uprising. They continue to fight for the liberation of the country.

One of these women's organisations, the All Nepal Women's Association - (ANWA) invited me to take part in a seven-week women's Campaign[1] (All Nepal Women's National Compaign) in the whole of Nepal. My husband was able to accompany me as a photographer.

During our journey from the end of February to the end of April 2002 the state of emergency meant constant danger for the restricted parliamentary democracy. With the approval of the parliamentary majority and the support of the U.S.A. the king has been terrorising the population since November 2001. This regime of terror against the population is conducted, of course, using the excuse of "fighting terrorists".

For ANWA this delicate political situation was no reason to cancel their planned Campaign but was a challenge to fight even more for women's rights. The determination of the women and the deep solidarity of the Women's Association with the mass of women and also with the liberation movement in Nepal impressed us greatly. At the same time our outlook was broadened because we were able to see the possibilities open to a strong international, fighting women's movement. We saw a lot of poverty but, above all, we saw people who fight this poverty, who fight the often still feudal traditions that discriminate against women and who fight for the liberation of women. We saw many women and children who did not collapse under the burden of oppression but who courageously believe in and want to fight for a better world, a world in which there is no more exploitation and oppression.

We experienced the strength of an organised women's movement and sensed what success the women's movement can achieve if it organises. Women beyond party limits and joins the workers' and liberation movements.

We also experienced that lobbyists and experts often active in so-called non-governmental organisations (NGOs) are not on the side of the people and do not support their struggle for a better future but with their projects and ideas just contribute to a stabilisation of existing conditions.

Through this report we hope that the strength and confidence of

---

1. *All Nepal Women's National Compaign (ANWNC)-The decision on the ANWNC was taken in the Fourth National Conference of ANWA Held in Butwal, Nepal in April 8-10, 2000. The decails about it is given in Appendix -D in page139.*

the women of Nepal will encourage many people to do as these women do and take their fate into their own hands. I would like to support the efforts towards a powerful women's movement which is closely linked with liberation movements and the workers' movement all over the world. Thus the example of Nepal does not only illustrate the wretched lives of the great majority of the population but at the same time the unbroken zest for life and the resistance to the inhuman conditions, the will to fight and the happy optimism of the people are inspiration.

That is why this is not just a book about Nepal but also a book to encourage all people, in whatever country they may live, to help build a bright future for us and our children so that the dream of a world comes true in which women's emancipation is reality and exploitation and oppression belong to the past.

September, 2002

Gabriele Beisenkamp

The Invitation to Nepal

It was November 2001 when the invitation from Durga Paudel, the then President of ANWA (All Nepal Women's Association) arrived. For two months my husband (as the photographer) and I were to travel through Nepal with a team of ANWA representatives in order to take part in their All-Nepal Women's Campaign. Why did I get this invitation?

I have been active in the women's movement in Germany for over ten years. For me the development of the movement is something really important and since the first meeting in 1997 I have supported the Women's Political Counsel with all my strength. The Women's Political Counsel has developed into a major forum of equal exchange of opinion and exchange of experience in the women's movement. In the year 2000 more than 2000 women, children and also men attended the 4th Women's Political Counsel. The fact that women from all over the world were involved in the discussions became an important feature of the Women's Political Counsel. Women from over 50 different countries met here.

Durga Paudel was one of these international guests and that is how we met in Germany. And now I was to go to Nepal to take part in their Campaign. I would soon be experiencing an exciting exchange of experience. In Nepal women have to struggle really hard for their formal equality and here in Germany we live in a country in which equality of women has formally been achieved but actual inequality between woman and man is becoming more and more apparent.

In her invitation Durga Paudel wrote :

We have honour to declare it that All Nepal Women Association (ANWA) is organizing two-year long All Nepal Women National Campaign-2001/2002. The objectives of this Campaign is

• to build countrywide public opinion to press the government to fulfill the legitimate demands of women,

• to awaken women to struggle for their rights,

(13)

• to organize them and to develop a strong women's liberation movement in the country ....

In the course of the Campaign women's meeting, mass meeting, seminar, wide public contact, signature Campaign in support of the legitimate demands of women etc. will be organized in various districts. Fraternal women delegation from foreign countries too are invited to participate in the Campaign. We are convinced that such a countrywide Campaign will play a historical rule in the women's liberation movement of the country....

The Fourth National Conference of the ANWA has proposed following two slogans for the liberation movement of women in Nepal.

1. Fight for equal property rights for women
2. Eliminate all discriminatory laws against women

That day I could not just carry on working calmly. I had thousands of thoughts in my head.

Is it possible to get two months' holiday?

Is my English good enough?

Can I meet the expectations that the women place in me?

What should I tell them about the life of women in Germany, about the women's movement?

And last but not least, what does the state of emergency in Nepal mean for our own safety?

But we had three months till we were due to leave and so we were able to sort out our questions and doubts bit by bit.

My husband and I went back to school. English teachers with international experience helped us to brush up our English because we were to communicate in English with the help of a translator. In Nepal itself the national language is Nepali but some 18 different languages are still spoken there today.

For a long time we wondered how we could give the women in Nepal a realistic impression of the lives of women in Germany. Because behind the facts of women's employment, number of children, child care facilities, divorce rates etc., there are personal fates, women who think

(14)

Some of the writers of the letters to the women in Nepal.

Letters from German women translated into Nepali and sold as a brochure, those letters met with great inerrest.

Beloyri (Kanchanpur), first meeting at a school playground.

Tribhuvan Basti (Kanchanpur), women self-confidently discuss old-fashioned traditions.

about their situations, women who think about private and social perspectives. We definitely did not want to confirm the false picture that everybody in Germany is rich and that the formal equality of women in Germany really means that women are liberated and that just a few small reforms are on the agenda. This is the picture that bourgeois politicians want to convey when they travel to these countries and it doubtlessly has an effect on the minds of the people there.

So we asked some friends and relatives to write letters to the women in Nepal in which they described their personal and social situations. But that was easier said than done. Insecurity and doubts had to be overcome first:

What have I experienced that I could tell women in Nepal?

When I write what I earn as a factory worker, won't the women in Nepal think: what else do these women want? They cannot know how expensive life is here.

In comparison to the poverty in Nepal we are well off; what will the women in Nepal think of us?

We sat together and talked and talked of course we have a higher standard of living than the people in Nepal. But Margit was able to give us a vivid description of her life as a factory worker. Every day she is greatly exploited at work and she is both mentally and physically exhausted.

And Ellen? She is on social security and has to be extremely careful with the low allowance she receives.

It became clear that our living conditions in a developed country are different to those in a developing country but that our struggle against exploitation and for the liberation of women is as justified as the struggle of the people in Nepal. With these letters we can give the people in Nepal a realistic picture of our conditions - an important basis to discuss things we have in common and to find a common way for a better future. The women were keen to get down to work and write their letters. We were able to go to Nepal with a whole folder full of letters in our luggage and thus a real thread came about in the international network. The letters were one of the most important contributions to this journey. Here is a small selection of the letters.[2]

---

2. All letters except those given here are given in Appendix-A, Page117.

Greetings from Germany

Dear women of Nepal,

I greet you warmly from the cold country of Germany. My name is Seyran and I was born in Turkey in Kurdistan. There I lived in a village and my grandparents had a farm. My mother only had a goat and a cow to make a living. Sometimes our grandparents supported us. The women played an important role in the families because they can do all sorts of work, also men's work, also what men cannot do. I am 36 years old and have been living in Germany for 22 years. My parents came here in 1963 as guest workers and I followed as a 13-year old with my 4 brothers and sisters. We lived alone with our grandparents for a year. In Germany I first had to attend a language course and then I attended junior high school. My brothers and sisters and I didn't want to stay in Germany. My sister and I then went to a boarding school for 4 years. This was a special school for foreign children and young people. We lived at the school and could visit our parents at the weekend. In that situation I noticed that I had to stand on my own two feet; my father was not interested in us.

At the boarding school I met many children from different continents. This was a very important experience for me. It was very exciting for me to get to know different cultures. (I learnt to speak Spanish and do Greek dances). We were girls only and grew very close. We all had similar problems and were able to support each other. There I did not feel like a foreigner; it was no problem if I pronounced something wrongly. During my apprenticeship as a joiner it changed. This was the first time that I became aware of a certain hostility towards foreigners here. My father could not understand that I trained to do a job which men usually do. I was lucky; it was the first time that there were more girl apprentices than boys. It was difficult for me to find a job in this profession. In total I only worked as a joiner for four years. The companies did not want to hire any women as joiners. I would actually have enjoyed continuing my education and getting the school leaving certificate and studying but I had to earn a living because my parents returned to Turkey. Three years ago I retrained as a media designer. Unfortunately I have not found a job. It is a very new profession. Companies try to attract computer experts to Germany with the Green Card although I and many colleagues here need a job. What they are doing means that there will be more applicants for the jobs.

The situation in my native country means that I have been interested and active in politics since an early age. The Kurdish people are not allowed to speak their own language, are not respected as people and do not have basic rights in Turkey. I want Kurdish and Turkish people to fight together for the rights of people in Turkey. I am curious to hear about your lives.

Long live international solidarity.

Seyran

Dear women of Nepal,

Today I met Gabi and would like to tell you a little bit about my life. My name is Ellen, I am 57 years old, have 5 grown-up children and two grandchildren. I am a housewife now. I have an illness which prevents me from working but on the whole I am well. I have a 2-room apartment with a bathroom and kitchen and during the week I live alone. My youngest son comes home at the weekend. He is in the army at the moment and not married yet. I am divorced and I raised my children alone. When I was young I attended school and then trained for 3 years as a machinist. After this I worked for some time and then thought that I should get married. I thought that with a family I would have a better life because my childhood and youth had been very hard. My father died in the war and my mother then had a partner who was unfaithful. But she stayed with him. I was married three times and at first did not know why my marriages had failed. I know that my husbands were to blame to a large degree but afterwards I realised that it also had to do with my inner attitude to men. I was no longer able to develop a normal relationship to men.

For me my children were and are the most important things in my life. Since my last divorce 12 years ago I have had to live on social security. I was a single parent with 5 children and could not find any work. But I really only gained a firm footing when I was able to go to work again and could take my life into my own hands again. Then fate struck again when I was unfortunately diagnosed with breast cancer. But after several operations and the courage to carry on, I overcame this. Today I am no longer able to work but otherwise I am well.

At the moment I get unemployment benefit and social security. However, the job centre checks regularly to see whether I am fit enough to work. Altogether I receive €537. I have to pay €350 for rent and heating and I have €287 to live off. This is really very little in Germany. But I still have my children.

I still hold my head high and hope that things do net get worse. I wish there was more solidarity among people. But even if I do sound a bit negative, I do not think that my life is negative even if it sounds a little like that. I just wanted to show you that even here in a rich country there are also many problems. Not everyone here benefits from the wealth of the country. Even if I cannot be active in Courage at the moment it has helped me very much to find my own way and has made me become responsible for my own problems.

I want you to know that as women you can achieve a lot. We must stick together as women, think positively and work for a better world. We must not neglect the men in our work though.

My very best wishes to you all. I wish you all a lot of strength.

Ellen

Dear women of Nepal,

My name is Brigitte and I am 51 years old, I have been married for 27 years and have two sons aged 24 and 32. In the 1960s the coal mines in Germany started to die. At that time both my father and my husband were working in the mines. The fight of the miners against the mine closures left its mark on me and influenced my life. First the miners were dismissed and then they had to leave their homes too. My parents also received notice for their apartment. But as a result of the miners' fight they were able to continue living there. The relatively low rent did not change either. The solidarity of the workers was impressive. Life on the miners' estates was like in a big community. Everyone knew everyone else and everyone helped everyone else. There was no envy among the people.

Since I got married I have worked as a cleaner. In the beginning I worked in the morning and the evening, so I had time for the children during the day. For three years I have lived alone with my husband. He has been a pensioner for 7 years. Seven years ago his aorta burst and he almost bled to death. The veins in his legs and heart area are porous. Since then he has had problems with his short-term memory.

Nevertheless, once or twice a week he goes to the flea market to sell things there. He cannot just sit at home all the time.

I have to carry on working because my husband has to take a lot of medicine and his pension is not very high. I also need medicine for my high blood pressure and cardiac arrhythmia.

I have known the MLPD (Marxist-Leninist Party of Germany) for 15 years and have been a member for 10 years. What I want for all people is socialism as a new society. I attended a course where I learnt about it and joined the organisation.

I am looking forward to hearing about your lives. I am interested to know how you cope with your lives and in particular to hear what life is like for women of around 50 years of age.

Yours sincerely,

Brigitte

Nepal : Poverty and Turmoil

On 24 February 2002 the day of our departure came at last: After a twelve-hour flight via Amsterdam with a stopover in the United Arab Emirates we finally landed in Kathmandu.

We received a warm welcome at the airport and were taken to Durga Paudel, the ANWA President. We were very glad that we were not alone. The first impression of Kathmandu is irritating. There are street traders everywhere; everywhere people try to sell things or offer services. The town made a very dirty impression on us. And they drive on the left! We would definitely have soon been run over by a taxi, cyclist or oxcart if we had not had our caring hosts with us.

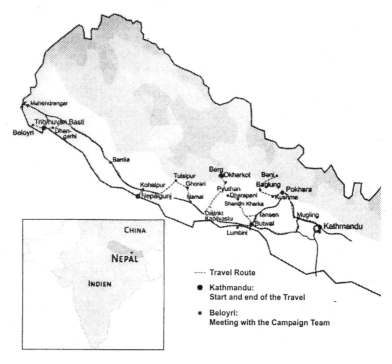

---- Travel Route

● Kathmandu:
Start and end of the Travel

● Beloyri:
Meeting with the Campaign Team

The highest point on the earth, Mount Everest

The hilly region: the mountainous area with altitudes of between 300m and 4500m

Terai: The lowlands and most fertile region in Nepal. 20 percent of the country is home to 50 percent of the population.

Wooden temple in Kathmandu

Kathmandu: A small girl is taken to the temple as the Kumari goddess.

We remembered what we had read about Nepal. With its 23.4 million inhabitants, Nepal is almost exclusively an agricultural country. The handcarts on which products are offered for sale gave a first impression of how the absence of industry forces peasants to work at a very primitive technical level. The many street traders and very small craftsmen's workshops in the streets let us guess in what way many people here have to earn their living. What sort of country is this, what is the history of this country that we are about to travel through?

A Short Look at the History of Nepal

In the 15th century some independent principalities such as Kathmandu, Patan and Bhaktpur were formed in the inaccessible mountain regions. The baoarders of Nepal were fixed by the borders that Nepal has today were only fixed in 1816 after Great Britain had invaded the country. In 1846 with British support the Rana family seized power and ruled with absolute power until 1951. Up to 1951 Nepal was hermetically closed to the rest of the world. With the support of the British the Rana dynasty exercised an oligarchic-feudal rule over the people. In 1951, with the support of India, the Rana dynasty was overturned in a popular uprising. The country opened up and a parliamentary, multiparty system was established which, however, was already removed again in 1960 by the feudal powers led by the king from the Shah dynasty. All political parties were banned, the opposition brutally persecuted. The hated Panchayat was established, a corrupt, brutal bureaucratic rule with King Mahendra as head. The Panchayat opened the country to shameless exploitation of the rich national resources by the imperialist powers. In 1990 the Panchayat system was finally overturned in a bloody 50-day uprising. But the king (Birendary had reigned since 1973) was not deposed. In 1991, under an interim government, a constitution was worked on for the first time and general elections prepared. In the 1994 elections the Communist Party of Nepal (United Marxist-Leninists - CPN (UML) emerged as the strongest party so that they were able to govern the country with a minority government. This did not suit the feudal powers around the king: nine months later the parliament was torn apart with military force and new elections were held in which the reactionary Congress Party of Nepal became the strongest party in the Nepalese parliament. Despite harassment and anti-communist Campaigns the CPN (UML) was the second strongest group in parliament. This constellation has not changed up to today.

In June 2001 King Birendara Shah and nine of his closest relatives were murdered. Up to now it has not been determined who was behind this bloody palace revolt. But Prince Gyanendra, the young brother of the murdered king, has definitely benefited because he became king just a few days after the murders.

On 26 November 2001 the new king announced a state of emergency which since then has been constantly extended. The state of emergency is aimed directly against the democratic rights and liberties of the Nepalese people and the activity of all democratic, anti-imperialist and revolutionary opposition forces. On the surface the state of emergency was proclaimed in order to take action against the Communist Party of Nepal (Maoist) which has proclaimed popular war for the whole of Nepal and which, in some regions, carries out armed operations.

Our experiences during our journey confirmed that the state of emergency is first and foremost directed against all progressive forces in the country. After our return to Germany we learnt from the media that parliament had been dissolved again and that new elections were to be held in November 2002.

Women's Struggle for Liberation - an Important Part of the History of Nepal

As long ago as 1951 ANWA, the women's association of the Nepalese Communist Party (Mashal) - NCP (Mashal) was founded in connection with the uprising to topple the Rana dynasty. At first we were rather confused by the fact that in Nepal several women's associations bear the name ANWA as a large number of progressive parties have given their women's associations this name. Because of the political development ANWA the women's organisation of the NCP (Mashal) was regularly forced to work secretly as were all other progressive and democratic forces. This, of course, made it much more difficult to organise women. For example, ANWA's second national conference in 1988 had to be held in India. So it was quite normal that ANWA played a major role in the so-called "anti-royalist movement" as well as in the struggle for democratic rights.

In early 1992 it once again became possible to work legally and in November 1992 ANWA passed a resolution to demand the same property

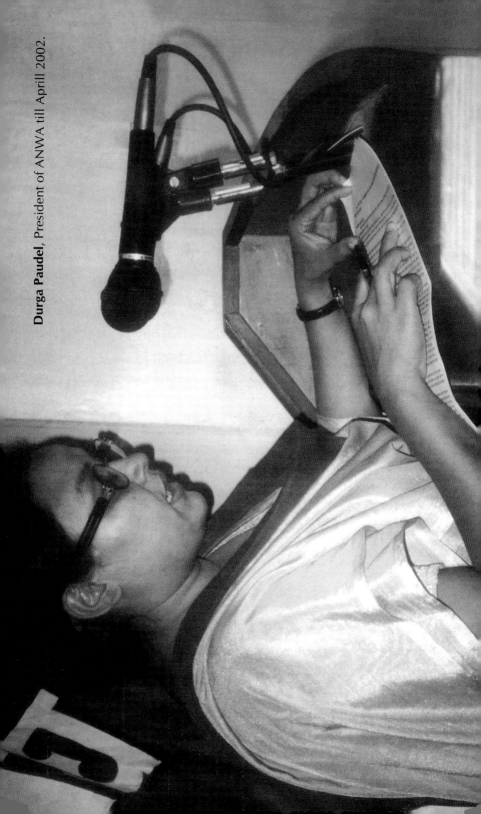

Durga Paudel, President of ANWA till Aprill 2002.

These women walked for six days (form Rukum and Rolpa) to attend the meeting (in Pyuthan)

Over four million Nepalese work abroad. Their families always wait them to come to home

rights for women. For the first time, not only in the history of ANWA but also in the history of the liberation movement of Nepalese women, a major demonstration for equal property rights for women was organised in the streets of Butwal, a large town in the south of country. Before the "Women's Rights Charter" was finally passed in 1995, ANWA organised several Campaigns on a local, regional and also central level in order to really study women's demands and to put them together in a declaration. Here is a small extract from the document:

"Men and Women, in principle are equal by birth. But they have been discriminated and victmized for long on different issues. They are almost in a stage of slavery. It Is, therefore, our historical responsibility to liberate them from such a grave situation with a view to giving them their long due self-respect and rights. Women's salvation is not an isolated issue, as it has its roots in the exploitative socio-political system. They can be liberated only when an exploitation - free society is created by eradicating the discriminatory system which deprives the working people the fruit of their labour and sacrifice. Women's condition as it is today is the direct result of the prevailing socio--economic system, which has been in practice for a long and it serves the interest of exploiting class. So, until and unless existing unjust socio-economic structure is not subverted, women can't realize basic change in their life. There are people in society who still object to giving equal rights to women in property. Similarly, some people oppose the women enjoying the rights of divorce, remarriage and widow marriage. But all these voices of opposition will disappear once the women raise the flag of revolt with full determination against all such practices. (..) Overhauling the present family system is one of the pre-requisites for the liberation of Women. It is this family structure which confines the women to household works and prevents them from expressing their feelings against the discrimination in the name of order."[3]

This preamble is followed by nine central demands which play a major role in ANWA's struggle. The first and most important demand is for equal property rights:

Durga Paudel reported how hard the women's association had worked to take these demands to parliament. !n 1995, for example, together with five other women's organisations they demonstrated inside and outside

3. Quoted from the Charters of Women's Rights.

the parliament for women's property rights. Nine women got themselves visitor tickets for the parliament and smuggled their banners unnoticed into the parliament building. At a suitable moment they unrolled their banners in parliament and called out their demands for property rights for women. The conservative parliamentarians were completely outraged; the women were immediately removed! A total of 105 women who were demonstrating outside parliament were arrested. But this did not deter ANWA from continuing their struggle for the rights and liberation of women.

While we were participating in the Campaign a law was passed in parliament giving women more rights. It became clear that parliament had to yield to the pressure of the women. A whole package of laws was passed which improves women's rights but, as ANWA says, is far from sufficient. So no reason for weakening the struggle. As the women of ANWA told us, the following was decided:

• In future, up to their marriage, women will have the same rights to the property of their parents as the sons. In the event of marriage they will still lose their right to this property.

• Up to now, in the event of a divorce, a woman had no property rights; it belonged exclusively to the husband. This has now been changed. However, the court still has an influence on whether a divorce becomes absolute.

• Up to now abortion has been illegal. Now, if both partners agree, abortion is possible within the first twelve weeks.

• Up to now, in the event of polygamy, men were gaoled for 1-3 months; the sentence is now 1-3 years.

• In some ethnic groups it was usual that the oldest brother would marry and that the wife then had to serve all the brothers, also sexually. This is now illegal.

These were Major successes of the women's movement in Nepal but by no means the goal in the struggle for the liberation of women.

We Meet the Campaign Team

After the first night at the home of Durga Paudel our journey started. First we had to travel right to the west of Nepal where we were to meet the Campaign team. After that we would move slowly towards Kathmandu

Children are always there

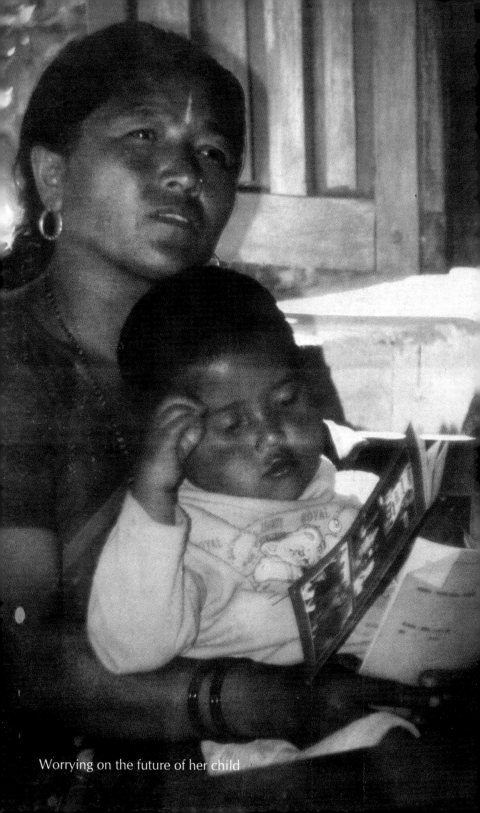

Worrying on the future of her child

where the final event was to take place. It was a two-day car journey to cover the 450 kilometres from Kathmandu to Beloyri, a small place in the far west of Nepal.[4] Two days full of new impressions. There was the Nepal "highway", the only east-west connection which the oxcarts, the rusty old lorries, a few cars and taxis, the motorcyclists and many mopeds but also buffalo herds and families of monkeys shared.

There was the kind family where we spent a night. The mother of our hostess sat down really close to me and stroked my arms, pulled my short hair and laughed. She had hardly ever seen women with pale skin and short hair.

There was our first meeting with Nirmala, the local ANWA activist who gave us a delicious meal and watched us closely to see what food we liked and what we did not like so much.

There were also the constant military controls which showed us: There is a state of emergency here! Before any bus or car could continue its journey, drivers and passengers had to get out , have their luggage checked and 500 metres further on they were allowed to get into the bus or car again. And all this took place under the eyes of soldiers with machine guns pointing. Only the fact that we were being accompanied by the member of parliament Dilaram Acharya from the National People's Front (NPF) prevented us from having to go through this procedure the whole time. Usually they looked at his identity papers and we were allowed to continue. Although the Campaign had been approved, it was only possible to run it through the permanent participation of members of parliament from the NPF who actively support the Campaign.

Like ANWA the NPF is a popular organisation of the NCP (Mashal). The NPF participates in elections and has five seats in the Nepalese parliament. In lots of towns we visited their small, public party offices and met their parliamentary representatives at lower levels. In two districts, for example, the Development Committee Chairman, the highest political representative of a district, was from the NPF. As the NPF does not focus on parliamentary work but fights locally and directly with people for their rights, it goes without saying that they actively support the Campaign.

Finally we arrived in Beloyri where we met four women from the ANWA central committee who travelled with us for the first 14 days to organise the Campaign.

---

4. Kanchanpur District.

At the start of the Campaign we were in western Terai. Terai is the flat region of Nepal on the border to India, the only part of Nepal in which industrialised agriculture can be carried out and is partly done.

The Campaign took us through 11 of the 75 districts of Nepal. Due to the state of emergency the route had to be changed before we started because in some districts it would have been too dangerous. And during the journey there were some surprises that led to changes. We started in the very west of Nepal in Mahendranagar and reached Kathmandu after seven weeks.

Important stops on our journey were: The district Tribhuvan Basti in western Terai: the industrial town of Nepalgunj on the border to India; the Dang district with its capital Tulsipur and the Tharu villages; the district Pyuthan with its magnificent mountain Okharkot; the mountainous district of Argha Khanchi with the biggest meetings; Kapilvastu - another district in Terai; Butwal one of the largest industrial towns in Nepal; the district of Baglung, the home district of Mina and Laxmi; the town of Tansen and, finally, Kathmandu.

It was a very full programme which took us to a different place nearly every day. The official programme scheduled various meetings which were planned in exact order in different places and towns.

Mass meetings, usually outdoors and in great numbers; so-called interaction meetings, indoor events in towns to which representative of other parties, women's organisations, representatives of NGOs and also individuals were invited. Here an exchange of experience and opinions took place.

In Butwal and Kathmandu two seminars were held and, of course, there were a number of press conferences.

Mina Pun

Mina is 28 years old, has been working for ANWA for ten years and has been on the central committee for two years. During the Campaign she was elected President of the women's association as the successor of Durga Paudel. Mina has three brothers and one older sister. When she was 14 years old, her parents and elder brothers organised her marriage. But she did not want the man they chose for her. She soon realised that

Members of the Campaign team, from left to right: Lila Maya Lamichhane, Mina Pun, Laxmi Baskota, Surya Thapa.

Kapilvastu district: "We struggled hard for our girls to attend school."

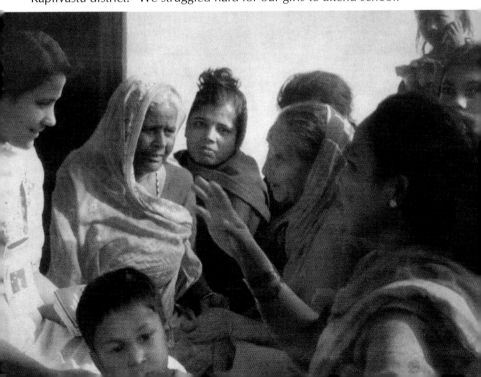

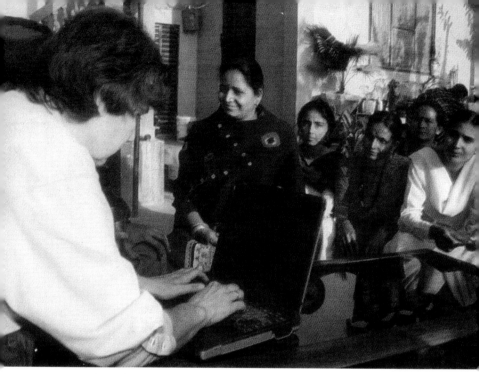

Nirmala Aryal, ANWA activist from Bansgarhi (Bardia) at an interview.

Campaign members washing the dishes.

women did not have the right to choose their own partner. Her father forced she to marry. So she agreed to marry but to this day has not moved into her husband's home. Their marriage has not been consummated. With no claim to land and without work she tried to get by. Later her father and older brother realised that it was a mistake to force her into marriage. After her father and elder brother died, her younger brother supported her and also gave her part of her father's property so that she could lead an independent life.

Mina's own experiences led her to become politically active at an early age. First she became involved in the youth organisation of the NCP (Mashal) and later she went to the ANWA. She is one of the few ANWA women whose livelihood is financed by ANWA. She travels almost the whole year to discuss the work with the local ANWA women, to help them, to win new women for the association and also to train them theoretically. At the meeting on International Women's Day, 8 March, it became apparent that Mina is not only an excellent speaker who can capture the hearts of women, she is also an authority on the lifework of Klara Zetkin (1857-1933), a German communist who was a passionate protagonist in the liberation of women.

Lila Maya Lamichane

Lila Maya is 49 years old, married and has five children. The other ANWA women lovingly call her "Aama" because she has an open ear for all the women and their problems. It was Lila Maya who always quickly disappeared when we came to a new place. We soon found her in the middle of a group of women. It was of great concern to her to speak to the women in the villages, to stand by them, to listen to their questions and problems and to advice them on how to tackle their work. She too has been in ANWA for ten years and two years ago she was elected to the central committee. Her husband is a farmer; he has asthma so that he can no longer work much. She has three sons and two daughters who are all married: At the age of 49 she already has twelve grandchildren. The sons live with her, as is the tradition, the daughters live in the families of their husband. Asked why she is active in ANWA, she gave the short answer: "I came to ANWA because I want a new society. I do not want any more exploitation."

Surya Thapa

Surya lives with her family in the capital Kathmandu. She is 50 years old, married and has an eight-year-old son. She has been an ANWA activist for 21 years and a member of the central committee for seven years. As for many women, it is quite normal for her to get up at 5 a.m., do the daily housework and then carry out her ANWA work. She was always there when something had to be organised. She took great trouble to meet all our wishes so that almost every day we gave a deep sigh saying: "Surya, please no extra service for us!"

Asked who was looking after her son while she helped to organise the Campaign, she said proudly: "My husband." He accepts the work she does at ANWA because he is active himself in the NPF. The son was now with her husband and she was sure that the two of them were managing well. This is definitely an exception in Nepal. She now works too, as she says, completely for ANWA. She used to be a teacher in a school of nursing.

Laxmi Baskota

Just like Mina, Laxmi comes from the mountainous region of Baglung. She is 28 years old and fights with all her strength for a socialist society. She has been active with ANWA for ten years, but before that was already in a youth organisation of the NCP(Mashal). At the age of 21 she was elected to the central committee of ANWA. She can tell a long story of what it means to be a woman in Nepal. One quiet evening she told us that she lives together with her mother and grandmother. Her mother had four children, "only" four girls. This really angered her father, who was a policeman, and he married another woman. Tradition gives him the right to do this because it is allegedly necessary for a man to have sons. But the new wife also "only" gave birth to a daughter. Under very difficult conditions, Laxmi's mother made sure that her daughters were able to attend school because she saw how important it is for girls to have a good education. Laxmi is very grateful to her mother for this. Today she works partly for ANWA and also tries to earn a living by working at the university. It was not until we arrived in the Baglung District that she told us that she also works there on the District Development Committee. This can be compared to the work of a member of the district council or even regional parliament in Germany. In the District Development Committee she brings forward the everyday problems of families and women; together with the women she fights for solutions, be it the electricity and water supply, be it the fight for a maternity home for young women, be it the problems of ethnic minorities.

We Learn How the People Live

The Campaign was prepared excellently. Without close solidarity with the people in Nepal it would not have been possible. Although most people had no telephone, the roads were often barely passable and the fact that the state of emergency led to changes in the course of the Campaign, the people were always prepared for us and we were warmly welcomed. There must have been lots of "secret" messengers whom we knew nothing about.

At meal times different families were always visited who all gave us really good food. Word quickly got round that we could not eat very well with our fingers and a fork and spoon were always waiting for us.

We spent most nights in private homes. Often children, and also adults, gave us their rooms so that we could sleep well. Every mosquito bite discovered on us in the mornings was a reason to make our next night even better. Mosquito nets were bought and the rooms carefully searched for mosquitoes. The length of the beds was measured because they were often too short for Thomas, my husband.

The fact that we and the ANWA activists usually spent the nights in private homes and also that the food was prepared by the families allowed ANWA to finance this Campaign and also gave us an excellent opportunity to really get to know the living conditions of the people and to live with them.

A Talk With Farmers

On the morning of 28 February we started off in Beloyri. On the very first day of the Campaign there were two meetings and at that point we did not yet know that we would be in a different place almost every day. In Tribhuvan Basti in the district of Kanchanpur, before we went to the next meeting, we were invited for a meal with the Chairman of the NPF of the district. Our journey was delayed, however, because the Jeep driver refused to cross a river. There was no bridge. He suggested that we should walk the last five kilometres if we wanted to use the Jeep for the rest of the Campaign.

They have been building a bridge over this river for years. It is not being completed though because the government has no money, explained the ANWA women. A small, makeshift bridge for bicycles and pedestrians has been built and is maintained by some young people. Anyone who wants to cross the bridge by bicycle or moped has to pay.

We grabbed the material, i.e. megaphone and brochures, we needed for the meeting and walked.

To make sure we were not hungry on the way. We were given sugar cane fresh from the field. And so the whole group walked along chewing sugar cane. We were closely watched to see whether we could eat the sugar cane correctly. The core of the sugar cane has to be sucked out and the fibre has to be cleverly spat out into the fields. I was obviously not yet very good at this because our Nepalese friends were very amused.

Eventually we arrived in Tribhuvan Basti and immediately 15 to 20 persons gathered there including the vice president of the farmers' organisation of the NCP (Mashal). Before we even arrived the rumour had spread that we were not keen on rice. We were able to correct the rumour later but now a roti, a type of bread, had been baked for us.

People were curious to know about farmers and their families in Germany and we were kept busy telling the people about farmers in Germany. The people at our little meeting found it hard to imagine that only two to three percent of the people in Germany work in agriculture, while in Nepal it is almost 90 percent. Luckily we had the letter from Wilma, a farmer, and were able to report on the life of a small farmer.

Wilma, who together with her husband runs a farm of 25 hectares, wrote to the friends in Nepal:

There are more and more regulations that farmers have to cope with. That means that you are either forced to keep a very large number of animals or you have to give up. When you need new equipment, you need financial aid because machines are very expensive and building costs very high. But only the very big farms get aid from the government.

An iron-smith in Pyuthan

A folk dance during Campaign.

A spontaneous comer meeting at Damdame (Pyuthan)

That means that you have to borrow money from the bank and then you are dependent on the bank. Normal farmers cannot work this way. Although our minister of agriculture, Ms Kunast, made us great promises, preference is given to the large-scale farming industry which has a lot of money. When you see how this works, it frightens me. Civil servants make decisions on new rules regarding manure and you have absolutely no influence. When I recently complained, the officer just laughed at me. My husband said that I should be careful as we are dependent on the agricultural office. But after three days it was still bothering me and I went to the office and complained. I said that I had got exact information from a relative who was a professor of agriculture at the university and he admitted defeat. Some days ago in the church choir in which I also sing, our priest collected signatures for a petition against the dismissal of 400 workers at a machine factory. I supported the petition because if the workers have to save on food, it will also affect us farmers.

They say that with a farm of 25 hectares it is difficult to survive in Germany - something that our Nepalese friends find difficult to imagine. Anyone who has 25 hectares in Nepal is a big landowner, a landlord.

The representatives of the farmers' organisation told us that in Terai they do not only produce agricultural products for their own consumption but are also able to supply the factory with sugar cane. Many farmers in Nepal cannot do this; they only produce for their own existence. But as there is only this one factory in the region, they have no other possibility to sell their sugar cane. They have no vehicles to drive the sugar cane somewhere else. This makes them very dependent on the one factory and the owner shamelessly takes advantage of this. He decides on the price and usually does not pay the farmers anything at all or only after a very long delay. The farmers are forced to borrow money from the bank in order to survive. The farmers' representative told us that this sugar cane factory was a joint venture project with India, i.e. a production co-operative of an Indian and Nepalese company. They no longer hope for any support from the government because the government does nothing against this form of exploitation of the farmers.

The dish washer

I talked to Mina about dish washers. What is a dish washer? What does it look like and what do you use it for?

(45)

I had the difficult task of explaining to her what a dish washer looks like and how it works. If only I had taken a few pictures of a kitchen with me. How can you explain all the technical aids that we now have in kitchens here?

We discussed the fact that it is not a luxury but that machines have become necessary in households because women go to work. The high percentage of women who go to work in Germany would not be possible without this technical equipment in homes. And, of course, it makes the boring task of housework much easier. It shows how technical progress can make our lives easier.

After our meal we were introduced to the Nepalese "dish washer". In front of the house there was a well; all the guests went to the well, wiped their cutlery clean in the sand and rinsed it with water. For the members of our Campaign it was clear that everyone cleaned their own cutlery, the men too. But in everyday life it is only the woman who do it. It is good for her if there is a well in front of the house. The drudgery that is forced on these women! In many mountain villages the women are even forced to fetch the water from a distant spring for cooking, washing, cleaning etc.

We used the journey to the next place to find out more about the conditions in agriculture. In the bumpy Jeep we heard that the "larger" agricultural firms are in this part of Nepal. There farm hands are employed or the landlords still have serfs. We were told that in Nepal there are around one million farm hands who earn 80 rupees, a bit more than one Euro, a day.

And of course: as a rule women earn up to 20 rupees less a day. The reason given for this is that religious tradition forbids women from using the plough. As they cannot do this difficult and responsible work, they cannot earn as much as the men. In Nepal, as in Germany, there is a justified demand for the same pay for the same work and this demand is voiced by ANWA.

As their pay is often not enough for them to survive, the farm hands are often forced, after ten hours' work, to cultivate a small piece of land for their own use and to keep a buffalo for their own survival. There is a contrast between old fashioned methods of production, such as a wooden plough with two oxen and agricultural machines such as tractors.

From the point of view of the people there is no acceptable reason for making the people work under these old-fashioned conditions. But for the landlord it is a simple calculation: Is it worthwhile for him to use agricultural machines or is he better off if he has lots of cheap farm hands working for him.

Visit to a Tharu Village

We had often expressed the wish to just go for a walk. This was never really understood because in Nepal it is a privilege to drive. When we were in the town of Tulsipur, we were granted our wish with a visit to a Tharu village. The Tharu are a tribe in Nepal that accounts for approximately 3.6 percent of the population. Often the people of this tribe still live under the conditions of serfdom. According to the ILO 14,000 people in Nepal still live under conditions similar to those of serfdom. The village of Kharchawa, which we visited on foot, consists of approximately 60 families with about 16 people each. The people are forced to work on the fields of the landlord and for this they receive food. They receive no wages!

Of course the people are not forced to live there. But what should they do, where should they go if there is nowhere else for them to work?

The living and working conditions reminded us greatly of the production conditions of the Middle Ages as shown in open air museums in Germany. But in Nepal these are the working conditions of the present.

There was the clay pit from which bricks were made by hand to build houses.

There were cow pats dried on roofs of houses to have fuel for the stove.

There were two large millstones with which the maize for the buffalo fodder was ground.

Apart from their almost 12-hour day on the landlord's fields the people have to grow their own crops on their own land of approx. 500 to 1000 sq.m. Often products grown on these fields are taken to the market so they can earn at least a little money to buy things essential to life. It was often the children who sold the products at the market instead of going to school.

(47)

Exploitation is not Worthwhile

The Pyuthan District is in the mountainous region of Nepal and can actually be reached via a difficult path also used by buses and lorries. The potholes on this path were so large that I was not always sure whether the Jeep would just tip over in one of the holes. Since I got to know these "roads" reports I read here in the newspapers that in Nepal a bus has again fallen into a valley no longer surprise me. Up to 20 years ago this district could only be reached on foot. Already here there are very high mountains and agriculture has to cope with very difficult conditions. The farmers have to plant small terrace fields in order to gain any usable agricultural area at all. There are only very few landlords in this area because the yields are mainly too low. Exploitation is not worthwhile.

In the torchlight - this small village does not have electricity - our host, a farmer, introduced himself and his family. Because Nepal is close to the equator, nightfall already comes at 7 p.m. The farmer told us about his daily struggle for survival. The family owns one hectare of land that they can cultivate, one cow and one buffalo. Seven members of the family have to live from this. The farmer and his wife, the son and his wife and their three children. The second son has already gone abroad because it is not possible to feed another family here.

They produce just enough to survive although three harvests per year (wheat, maize, rice) are possible. They only have very primitive production methods as they do not have the money to buy anything else. The grain is harvested stalk for stalk with a simple sickle.

They have no possibility to sell any of their produce. On the one hand there is no market that they can get to and, on the other, they do not produce enough. Their only chance to earn money is occasionally to sell a cow or a buffalo. This money has to be enough to buy everything they cannot produce themselves.

The Credit Co-operative

Our hosts for the night told us that the farmers from the area had formed a credit co-operative. A total of 37 farming families pay in 20 rupees each a month. The money is managed by them. In this way they are not dependent on any bank and the interest that they pay helps them.

Women working on road consturction.

Many women earn their living by smashing stones to make gravel.

Kusmi Shera (Baglung), wood is often sawn manually.

Shoemaker in Pyuthan.

Nobody grows wealthy through this co-operative but all of the money is at their disposal. This credit co-operative is an important facility for these families allowing them to make purchases or to cope with shortages. Whoever needs money receives a loan for six months but has to pay 18 percent interest. If the loan is not repaid after six months, the interest increases to 36 percent. The farmers tend to be very strict with themselves.

But our host did not just want to tell us about his living conditions and during breakfast the next morning he asked us about the state of the German workers' movement:

What do the people think about the reunification? What Marxist-Leninist parties are there in Germany and, above all, how many? How and with what means do the people in Germany fight for their social liberation? Questions that we had not expected but were happy to answer. Breakfast took somewhat longer and we had to hurry to get to the next meeting on time.

Hardly any Industrial Development

We had not expected to see any industry in the mountainous regions of Nepal; that is why we looked for it all the more in the Terai. Because the women told us again and again that one of their biggest problems is that there are no jobs in Nepal. A very large number of people are forced to leave their families. The men are forced to work abroad and can, at the most, only visit their homes once a year or maybe even once every two years. Often they earn so little that they can hardly send any money home.

In Nepalgunj, one of the few large towns in the Teraj and close to the border with India, we were able to discover an industrial area. But all we saw were closed factories. The representative of the NPF told us that these factories were no match for international competition and had been ruined. The development of industry had been destroyed particularly by India through unilateral trade agreements. India, for example, is interested in exporting products to Nepal but hardly interested in importing anything from Nepal. There are no limits on imports from India. But there are high duties on exports from Nepal to India. Up to now, they said, India had successfully prevented the development of a vehicle manufacturing industry in Nepal. All lorries, all agricultural machines that we saw were imported from India. Through the geographical situation of Nepal, which borders on India on three sides and is separated from China in the north by the mountain range, it is very difficult to develop trade independent of India. Development of their own industry is actually prevented. Nepal has a large foreign trade deficit. Imports are three times as high as exports. In 1997 India was the biggest importer to Nepal accounting for 27 percent of the imports.

And so lots of small businesses are developing in Nepal through which people try to survive. Along the streets in the towns and villages there are lots of repair workshops for the small number of agricultural machines, lorries and cars.

Apart from India, Germany and the U.S.A. are Nepal's most important trading partners. In 1997 the largest number of exports went to Germany, a total of 34 percent, the carpet industry accounting mainly for this. In 1997 the U.S.A. was in second place. As far as imports are concerned, India is in first place at 27 percent followed by Hong Kong at 15 percent and Japan at 11 percent.

Tourism is becoming more and more important for Nepal. In 1995 48 percent of foreign currency proceeds came from tourism (170 million US dollars). Almost one third of the tourists came from India, while about every sixth tourist came from the U.S.A. Germany and France.

Nepal's Carpet Industry

According to official figures, 150,000 people, mostly young women and girls, currently work in Nepal's carpet industry although many small factories are not registered. According to estimates of the ANWA representatives, up to 250,000 people work in the carpet industry which is completely dependent on the import of raw wool. In 1999 75 percent of the production went to Germany, 9 percent to the U.S.A. and the remaining 16 percent to Switzerland, Great Britain, Belgium and Austria.

The word "industry" immediately made me think of a large factory. I had to think differently though to get some idea of Nepal's carpet industry, a major sector of the economy. The factories are generally small rooms in which in very cramped space there are several looms at each of which two or three women or girls work.

It was very difficult to arrange a visit to one of these "factories". Our ANWA women really had to use the art of persuasion. The small factory owners were very scared that we were representatives of NGOs checking their factories for child labour. The ANWA representatives explained to us that in the years 1992/93 several NGOs had a Campaign against child labour. This led to a far-reaching collapse of production. The German trading partners only wanted to buy carpets that had not been produced by children but, of course, they did not want their profit margin to change. All the pressure was put on the small carpet factories. They should employ adults but, at the same time, sell the products at low prices.

It seems that the whole development just drove a large part of the carpet industry into illegality. For example, in the Nepal 2000 yearbook issued by the Institute for Integrated Development Studies, it says that just 240 factories are properly registered but that there are at least 1,000 such factories.

In the registered factories, it says, child labour has fallen to one percent. The report continues that in Nepal an estimated 2.6 million children work, i.e. half the Nepalese children fit for work. This clearly shows that the NGO Campaigns have, in fact, changed nothing in actual child labour. On the contrary, because of the conditions in Nepal many families are dependent on their children working; without their income the families would not be able to survive. In this situation the representatives of ANWA said that they are not generally opposed to child labour but that they aim to improve the working conditions. The children are often the only members of their families who, by working in the carpet factories, earn any money at all. This is a struggle which the families, the children and also ANWA or other organisations have to develop and conduct. They see this as a step towards making themselves strong against capitalist exploitation. They were very sceptical regarding the Campaign that was organised over their heads from outside: "Why don't they work together with us?" they rightly ask.

The experiences of the socialist People's Republic of China in the 50s, 60s and 70s showed on the basis of the abolition of exploitation of people by people: It is sensible to involve children in social production in accordance with their level of education and abilities. In this way they can learn at any early stage to take responsibility for social development and what they learn at school is closely linked to their concrete experiences.

Visit to a Brickworks in the Kathmandu Valley

In the Kathmandu valley we had the opportunity to visit a rather large brickworks. The evening before our ANWA friends organised a very interesting discussion for us with the local trade union members. This trade union organisation is also an organisation of the NCP (Mashal). Just as with the women's organisations, the trade union organisations in Nepal are usually connected to a party which means that every party has its own trade union.

The local trade union chairman told us that this brickworks had been built in 1967 with the support of the People's Republic of China and had been state owned since 1970. At that time about 400 workers were employed there. The development of this industry at that time also led to the development of a trade union movement in the whole valley and a struggle of the people for elementary social benefits, for example, a company pension scheme because in Nepal the state pension system is by no means sufficient. The state pension is 2 Euros a month from the age of 70.

We had an important and exciting discussion here on our experiences of non-partisan trade union and also women's work and how important it is to defend the non-partisan status. Because we think it would be very difficult to conduct a struggle for concrete improvements in working conditions or against exploitation if the employees are organised in different trade unions: How do you carry out a common struggle here but also the discussion on different ideas? It became apparent that it is really not easy. We were able to describe the experiences in Germany in the struggle for the unified trade union. In the 1920s the reformist trade union leadership in Germany had started to fight against the growing influence of the Communist Party of Germany (CPG) in the trade unions by the mass expulsion of communists. The revolutionary Trade Union Opposition then formed by the CPG was meant to group together the trade union members who had been expelled. But more and more independent, red trade unions developed from this. When Hitler seized power the trade unions were smashed. Many Social Democrats and Communists met again in the concentration camps.

District capital Baglung: Bricks are produced manually.

Road construction.

Lentils being threshed by hand.

Kathmandu valley: even in the semi-mechanised production at a large brickworks, lots of work is still done manually.

Because of these experiences after the war most trade unionists demanded the formation of really democratic unified trade unions. Our accounts met with great interest.

Privatisation of Nepal's State Industry

Since the 90s systematic privatisation has taken place in Nepal; most state businesses have been sold to foreign companies. The Nepalese government also encourages further privatisation of state companies via the internet. For the year 2000, for example, the sale of the Nepal Tea Development Corporation, the Butwal Power Company and three cement factories was offered. This privatisation just sells off the national economy and means greater dependence on international companies which buy up these industries. Is this the way to help Nepal recover from its huge debts which in 1977 were 2.4 billion US dollars? In 1995 Nepal already spent 59 million US dollars on repayment of debts. The debts are paid and the people starve.

In 1993 the brickworks we visited was also privatised, accompanied by a real worsening in working conditions. The trade union members told us about the methods used to persuade the workers to buy shares to redevelop the allegedly bankrupt factory. By purchasing shares the employees were to produce a total of 25 percent of the capital to be invested. This was done by 95 percent of them. Since then neither the wages nor the "dividends" have been paid to the workers punctually.

Just like in Germany they should work as hard as they can for the well-being of the company that allegedly has to repay more in interest than profits that it earns. And the working conditions got much worse. Although some 400 workers are still employed at the works only twelve colleagues have binding employment contracts. The large majority are contract workers or day labourers. The contract workers receive short-term agreements depending on how many orders the firm has, the day workers are forced to offer their labour every day and they do not know whether and on what day they will actually be able to work. Because of these experiences the trade unions are now above all fighting against further privatisation and contract labour.

It became clear that not only in the women's movement an international exchange of experience and a common struggle are necessary but also in the trade union and workers' movement. When we visited the brickworks the next day, together with the trade union representatives we were able to roughly calculate that the brickworks actually has a daily turnover of approximately 200,000 rupees with wages coming to 35,000 rupees. Costs of material are low because the clay comes directly from the area next to the brickworks.

Through the State of Emergency the Rulers are Trying to Break the People's Wish for Freedom

We can imagine that in the long term people will not put up with such poverty. And it was again on one of the long Jeep rides that we learnt more on the significance and firm establishment of the revolutionary movement in Nepal. Our ANWA representatives reckoned that the majority of the population supported the idea of socialism. The geographical proximity to the formerly socialist China was one of the reasons for the broad Marxist-Leninist movement in Nepal.

But our next question was: why is this movement so split? In Nepal there are around ten parties which describe themselves as left-wing or revolutionary parties but which in practice have very different policies. The representative of the NCP (Mashal) had to go back in time because there is not just one reason for this.

Parties have only been allowed in Nepal since the 90s. Most of the time they had to work illegally. Also there were hardly any roads, telephones, postal service or similar facilities in Nepal. How could there be a real discussion if parties were banned or it took six days to walk to the nearest district? Basic discussion on major international developments could not easily be held and certain differences of opinion could not be settled.

He told us that most people agreed that the Soviet Union had left the socialist path at a very early stage; it was more difficult to agree on the development in China. His party, for example, was of the opinion that after the death of Mao Zedong China had also left the socialist path. But the revolutionary parties have very different ideas on the way Nepal should take to become independent of other countries and introduce socialism.

(58)

In many parts of the country the crops are threshed by buffalo.

The only through east-west road in Nepal, thus called "highway".

A girl with a load of wheat plant.

Typical farmhouse.

In the German press the broad revolutionary trend in Nepal, its firm position among the population and the unbroken will for freedom of the people is not mentioned and in Germany the impression is given that it is just the CPN (Maoist) that murders throughout the country.

Of course we wanted to know the truth about the CPN (Maoist) which, according to official statements, is the reason for the state of emergency. We were told that this group is relatively strongly represented in three to four districts of the country and also has military camps there. The people whom we met did not like this group. They told us about attacks at night in which the CPN (Maoist) representatives forced people to give them money and food. They also spoke of rape - the women and families locked themselves into their homes every night. We were also seriously warned to lock ourselves into our rooms every night. While we were in Nepal there were many armed incidents between the military and this group. When we were visiting Durga Paudel's brother near the district capital of Kapilvastu there was no electricity and the telephone did not work. Her brother told us that just a few days before the people from the CPN (Maoist) had destroyed the telephone and electricity connections to be able to fight the military more easily.

The representative of the NCP (Mashal) told us that this group had a great deal of money with which they had tempted a large number of criminal elements to join them.

The fact that these people mistakenly describe themselves as followers of Mao Zedong is shown in a short quotation by Mao Zedong in which he describes the relationship of Marxist-Leninists to the masses:

"Zitat aus AW III, S.216/217 deutsche Ausgabe"

Is the state of emergency really only directed against this group or is it rather a matter of breaking the wish for freedom of the people? On 27 March 2002 the newspaper Frankfurter Rundschau wrote: ... according to amnesty international 3,300 people, including many lawyers, journalists, students and teachers, have been arrested on suspicion of being members or sympathisers of the Maoist underground organisation. According to many Nepalese observers the inexperienced army is very reckless, people are tortured, relatives receive no information ...."

We made experiences that confirm this report. The state of emergency is indeed directed primarily against the people.

The Journey Stops Here

After a successful meeting in Tribhuvan Basti we wanted to continue to the next place. But this was not possible. The military prevented us from continuing our journey; and I must admit, I did not feel too comfortable in this situation. Exactly one day earlier the military had used elephants to destroy the houses of a whole village. What was the reason?

25 years ago the villagers occupied the land and since then they have been cultivating it. The government now says: either the people have to buy the land or leave it. But they do not have the money to buy it.

In Nepal there is a common law according to which land that has been occupied for twelve years can be kept. The people were very angry, they said that they would rather be shot dead by the military than leave their land. They have no other perspective. The representative of the NPF accompanying us thought that the state of emergency was being used to take action against these people because in a state of emergency any protest against or public criticism of the government or military is banned. Nevertheless the people have no other choice than to take up the fight for their lives.

A Village is Burnt Down

Unfortunately this was not the only experience of this kind. Two weeks later when we had left the district capital of Kapilvastu, we met people outside the place whose village had been burnt down by the military the night before.

As we stood speechless by the smoking pile of ashes, saw the people and all the children who were now homeless, Durga Paudel told us that this was the fourth time in 14 months that these people's huts had been burnt down.

What is the reason for this? It has nothing to do with the fallow land that the people had occupied to scrape a living. With the support of ANWA and the NPF but with no electricity or water supply these people build their huts in order to scrape a living through growing food.

Durga Paudel told us that a former minister of agriculture had illegally taken possession of this 100 hectare piece of land and with the help of the military he has it cleared again and again because he says it is his property that has to be protected.

The will to survive, the optimism of these people is incredible. They were all so busy in their burnt down village. The belongings that they had managed to save were put together, the ash was swept away and they immediately started to rebuild their huts.

That day it started to rain really hard and I kept thinking of these people. How will they get through tonight and the coming nights? Will they manage to rebuild their huts, to cultivate the land?

But at the same time I had to think of these people's links with ANWA and the NPF. They are not alone. They have been conducting their struggle together for four years and they can count on the support of the population. These are very good conditions for success in their fight to settle on the land.

As we learnt the next day, in this district ANWA concentrates its work on helping these landless families to build up an existence. ANWA has made public the illegal appropriation of the land and private enrichment by the former minister and this year the matter will be dealt with by the Supreme Court.

Here too the state of emergency was used to take action against the people. True to the motto: No resistance!

The People's Will to Fight is Unbroken

We had more experiences during our stay in Nepal:

• Members of the Campaign team were beaten up.

• Farmers who were still working on their fields after the curfew were shot dead; the newspaper wrote: "Maoist shot dead."

• Four members of the National People's Front in Baglung District were arrested and murdered.

• In the mountains of Baglung is a place called Kusmi Shera. It cannot be reached by car. The only connection is a narrow path. It was forbidden to use mules to transport food there, allegedly to starve out the CPN (Maoist).

Here we often read in the newspaper that a state of emergency has been called to "fight terrorism". But we never read that the reason for the state of emergency is to intimidate the people and to silence progressive forces. The USA has already included Nepal in its so-called "war against terror".

Gradually we heard some of the facts. For example, US President Bush includes Nepal as one of the critical countries on the margin of his "axis of evil" and is already making a package with weapons, ammunition and other military equipment. The USA wants to spend around 200 million dollars on this and an accompanying "social" package. Secretary of State Colin Powell visited Nepal and offered American support in the fight against "terrorists". The Nepalese military is advised directly by members of the US armed forces and a US military base is being prepared in Nepal. Representatives of the NPF told us that up to now the Nepalese parliament had rejected the USA's suggestion to set up a military base. Is the people's wish for freedom now to be broken with the help of the USA?

We saw the people's will to fight in Nepal. We are sure that the rulers will not succeed in suffocating this deep wish for freedom and a better life. We were angry and rather naive when we publicly protested at meetings in Nepal against this "terror" against the people and encouraged the people to continue their struggle for liberation.

Before we reached Butwal to hold a large meeting in a hall, our representative from the NCP (Mashal) took my arm and said I should be a bit more careful today in my protest against the state of emergency. He said that here in the town they did not know who would be coming. I was a bit irritated at first but then I suddenly realised that my public, open protest had endangered our own safety and that of the whole team.

It is part of the success of this women's Campaign that it took place at all - despite the state of emergency because it was the only public, political action in this period of state of emergency in Nepal. The Campaign did not only encourage women not to give up under any circumstances; it was encouragement for the whole population in this part of Nepal. For the people it was not always easy to decide whether to attend the meetings because they never knew what would happen, whether they would encounter a military control or similar. According to estimates of the ANWA women approximately 20,000 people took part in this Campaign and showed that they would continue to fight against exploitation and oppression. Some women even walked for six days to attend a meeting. This shows their deep ties with the movement and also their tremendous wish for liberation.

Nepal's Women Rise Against Exploitation and Oppression

Our vehicle, the Jeep, did not only transport our luggage but sometimes up to 19 people. I would never have thought this possible before. But we already learnt our first lesson the day after we arrived when we were asked to reduce our two suitcases to one because there was no room for more. Now we knew why.

The first meeting we attended was in the extreme south-west of Nepal, in Beloyri. From there we went through eleven districts back to Kathmandu.

The first meeting, attended by about 150 women children and also men, was held at 9 a.m. in the schoolyard in Beloyri. They all wanted to hear what ANWA had to say, why they supported property rights for women and also what they thought about the state of emergency. We were overwhelmed by the wonderful reception and the great interest in the development in Germany. We were completely surprised that the local newspaper wanted an interview after the meeting.

After this, unfortunately, there was hardly any time to talk to the women because at 3 p.m. on the same day there was a meeting in Dhangarhi attended by over 200 people. And before the meeting we were, of course, invited to eat in a Tharu village.

We were surprised at the great interest in these meeting. On the very first day 350 people had come to the meetings. This was a normal working day during the state of emergency. How many would have come if there had not been a state of emergency?

We told the women from ANWA how happy we were that so many people had come. Their answer was: "Here in the west we are just starting to develop our work, here we are not yet so well represented."

This made us very curious about what was to come. We were also very happy about the great warmth with which we were received. This was the first time that a foreign delegation was visiting the women in their villages. They told us that representatives from foreign NGOs and parties often come to Nepal. They attend congresses in Kathmandu or other towns and then leave. But they had never seen that foreign guests take part in their daily lives and are involved in a Campaign like this throughout the country. They really admired us for the fact that we were doing this in the current difficult political situation.

Patience Needed to Fight Feudal-patriarchal Traditions

We only really understood during the Campaign why one of the major aims of the Campaign was to create public awareness of the justified demands of women. What they had written in their charter for women's rights was so normal for us. But gradually we got to know the traditions with the help of which the special oppression of women is organised. They mainly have their roots in feudalism and are firmly established among the population through religion. At the meeting in Tribhuvan Basti, for example the ANWA women tried to convince those present that the following custom is wrong:

During menstruation women and girls have to leave their families because they are "unclean". If they are lucky a small shelter has been built for them outside the village and they can stay there until their menstruation is over and they can return to their families.[5] If their children are still very young, their mothers take them with them but if they are older they stay with the family. Until I went to Nepal I had never heard of such customs and I could hardly believe that such things still exist today.

They also told us about the so-called daughter sacrifice which is part of the Hindu religion. This is the cult of the virgin Kumari. Here young daughters, often aged between three and four, are selected by priests and taken to a temple to live as young women married to God. When their menstruation starts, the girls have to leave the temple. The Kumari loses her position and returns to her family. Afterwards the lives of these girls

---

5. *The custom is in the hills of for West Nepal. In other parts of Nepal during menstruation women can live in the house, but have to remain untouched with any male.*

are anything but divine because usually these women do not find husbands. Men fear the alleged supernatural power of these young women. As Kumari they have not attended any school so that it is very difficult for these women to earn money. The ANWA women told us that it is not unusual for these girls to end up as prostitutes because they have no other way to earn a living.

When we were in Kathmandu some weeks later we saw a young girl being taken to the temple. As we knew the background, the celebrations did not make us feel happy at all.

In the course of time we learnt a few sayings that really reflect the traditions that are so hostile to women. And we were able to understand more and more that it is necessary to create public awareness for the justified demands of the women. I would like to reveal some of the sayings to readers:

- If a son is born it should be celebrated by slaughtering a goat; if it is a daughter, a pumpkin is enough.

- Let it be late, but let it be a son.

- The birth of a son paves the way to heaven.

- The wife is the dust on your foot.

- If a woman rules the house, you can be sure that it will be destroyed.

- A son lights up the whole world, a daughter just the kitchen.

I brooded over the reason why these feudal-patriarchal traditions still have such an effect seeing that it would be no problem just to reject them. To read on the journey I had taken the book "New Perspectives for the Liberation of Women" by Stefan Engel and Monika Gartner-Engel. This book was a true companion because I was able to use it for reference when I wanted to clarify for myself certain aspects, connections and background of my experiences: Here is a quotation on my question:

"One of the most significant consequences of imperialist exploitation and oppression is the conservation of feudal and semi-feudal structures, customs and moral concepts. They impede all social progress in many capitalist societies of the developing countries which are clients of imperialism. In particular, in the personal life circumstances of the

(67)

masses they function as onerous fetters, mainly for women. These feudal remnants do not by any means disappear by themselves when capitalist relations of production are introduced, but are in part purposely maintained as instruments of the reactionary rule of imperialism, or are even systematically extended.

The feudal-patriarchal oppression functions up to this day on the basis of an entire system of laws, religious traditions, everyday customs and ideas about morality."

It has also become apparent that in particular the Nepalese Congress Party, the reactionary government party was a keen advocate of these reactionary traditions regarding women.

The Fight Against Polygamy

Although it is illegal and since recently has been punishable by up to three years' imprisonment, in Nepal there are still men who have several wives. For some men it is a status symbol to be able to afford several wives. Another reason for a man to take a second wife is if the first wife has not given birth to any sons. The sayings quoted above clearly showed the preference given to sons. The material background for this is that the birth of sons represents the old age insurance of the older generation. Daughters leave their parents' homes, sons stay and look after the older generation. This is one of the reasons why these traditions have remained so long in rural areas.

ANWA works intensively against these traditions everywhere where women are confronted by them. More than once I was able to observe that after meetings young women went to ANWA representatives and told them in tears that since their husbands have had second wives, they have been beaten. They wanted concrete advice and help from the ANWA women, something that can only be offered if there is a strong group in that place that deals with this problem. In concrete cases contact was made to the local ANWA representatives who then tried to help these women.

The right to divorce and, above all, own property rights is particularly important for these women. These rights would at least give them a legal possibility and, above all, a material basis to escape from their humiliating role. In her letter to the women in Germany, Laxmi's mother talked about this from her own experience. The small widow's pension that she has received since the death of her husband is divided between two women. She cannot live from this.

Dear German Women friends,

Warm Greetings!!

I wish to express my hearty greetings to all women of Germany on the occasion of Happy New Year 2059 (According to Nepalese Calendar)

My name is Meena. I am 52 years old. I live in Baglung district of Nepal. We do not have property right for women therefore, many women are illiterate. Children are not treated as equal in our society. Every sector male have dominant role. Every aspect of our society women are in a backward condition. Nepalese women face these severe problems. Our government does not pay any attention. If government had paid a little attention towards women's problems the present situation would not have come, because there is also possibility to improve the situation within the political system. I work in a town community of All Nepalese Women Association (ANWA) in Baglung District. This association struggles for economical, political, social, religious, education equal opportunity for women. As a result of our struggle we are able to get some improvements in the women's conditions. These improvements are not enough for us. We must struggle more for more rights. In our society daughters are looked down. To give birth of daughter is also looked down, we have tradition that son is considered as everything. I chose my husband myself. I have four daughters. Since I gave birth only daughters, my husband married a another women. I faced difficulties to care of my daughters, but I struggle to send my daughters to the school. In the name of the property I have a little house. My husband died 16 years ago. Something has changed in the condition of property of my family. Our country is agriculturalist. The agricultural technology is primitive type. Many people are unemployed; therefore many youth have left to foreign country to work.

In this present condition, our country is under the state of emergency. People have difficulties for their survival. In this context our women's organisation has carried out the national Campaign. In this Campaign comrade Gabi and Thomas have been participating to build solidarity between Nepalese and German women's movement. We are very happy for the letter you sent, which helped us to understand the status of women in Germany. For this reason we thank Gabi, Thomas and all of you. I wish similar kind of solidarity in future as well.

Yours Sincerely Meena Baskota.

Convincing People to Marry for Love

We were completely surprised when Mina Pun told us, that even today around 80 percent of marriages in Nepal are arranged. Even many of the ANWA women we met had arranged marriages. Parents usually look for a partner for their child when the child is still very young. When menstruation starts it is time for a girl to get married. It was not unusual to see 15-year-old girls who were already married and had children. Every time I saw such young women already married. I had to think of our own daughter who is now 16 years old. I could not imagine, nor would I really think her capable of already being a mother. And she would definitely not like me to pick a partner for her.

Very slowly the age at which girls in Nepal marry is rising and the average age for girls to marry is now 18.1 years.

ANWA has been very concerned with this issue and in its Charter of Women's Rights,[6] it supports a very progressive position which is not undisputed in Nepal. It says:

'The present marriage system is based in favour of men and so this is responsible for many ills and miseries in the life of women. In the name of marriage women have been facing all sorts of insults and humiliation for centuries. Women don't have outlets to escape from the trauma of divorce and other problems related to marriage. When married life becomes like a hell, then there should be provision for getting rid of such condition. In this regard the following points should be taken into consideration:

• Marriage should be based on mutual love and feelings for each other and nothing should be done against the wishes of one party.

• Marriage based on caste and religion must be banned and eliminated.

• Conjugal life should be based on mutual love, respect equality and freedom.

---

6. *The full text of the document, Charter of Women's Rights is given in Appendix-C, Page 131.*

- In case of discriminatory behavior and injustice inflicted on her by her husband and his parents, she should be entitled to divorce or remarriage.
- Divorce process should be very easy and inexpensive.
- Women should have rights over the ownership of property even after the divorce or remarriage.
- After divorce, there should be a provision for children's livelihood and education based on justice without any discrimination against women keeping in view of the supreme interest of the children's future.

A lot of work also has to be done to convince ANWA women of these very progressive demands. Because they too are affected by the old traditions and moral ideas through which the oppression of women is better established than through obviously reactionary laws.

In the Baglung district we were able to speak personally to a small group of women. With just a few exceptions, all of their marriages had been arranged. Proudly they told us that they ask their children whether they agree to the choice of partner. They would never force their children to marry against their will.

They were a little unsure when they asked us whether we helped our children at all in finding a partner and whether the children could really do this alone.

An elderly woman smiled at us and chuckling she told us that she was in favour of love marriages. She said she had married for love and not taken the caste system into consideration. She was very happy, she said, that we had the same opinion.

For girls in Nepal it is very important that they get married because their whole livelihood and support depends on this. Women do not usually have a profession and without any property rights they are completely dependent on the new family. So the careful choice of the daughter's future family is a very important decision in her life.

In the Pyuthan district we also had the opportunity to discuss this issue with a group of women. For many of them it was completely normal to arrange their daughter's marriage; their prestige would suffer if, for example, their daughter married someone from a lower caste. They also felt responsible for their daughter's future.

(71)

The same day we were able to visit the Kul Bahdaur family in Okharkot. They are members of the lowest caste, the untouchables.

The division of the population into groups with different social statuses originated in Hinduism. 90 percent of the population of Nepal is Hindus. They are divided into castes. Knowing what caste a person belongs to, tells you something about the person's eating habits, possibly jobs, behaviour and status, although this is not as strict as in India. The four original classes are, in order, the priests (Brahman), warriors (Kshatriya), the working population (Vaishya) and the servants (Shudra). The untouchables (Dalit) are not included in this order. These castes have subdivided into a large number of groups still existing today.

The family of Kul Bahadur was very happy that we visited them and with the help of our translator they told us about their lives. The 38-year old daughter-in-law lives with them with her children. She is one of the many women in Nepal who live with their parents-in-law without their husbands because they are working abroad and only come home every eighteen months at the most. He only sends money if he can give it to a friend and be sure that it will arrive. She only attended school for two years.

Often the families of the lowest caste are workmen. At the age of 80 Kul Bahdaur still had to make and repair tools in order to feed his family. He has to collect the charcoal he needs in the woods himself.

Asked what the family thinks of love marriages, the 80-year old immediately said that he is in favour of love marriages. The young people, who had joined us in the meantime, were obviously embarrassed and it took a while before they admitted that they were also in favour of marrying for love.

This is an interesting observation: If no consideration has to be paid towards property it is possible to choose a partner you like. I remembered that in his book "The origin of the Family, Private Property and the State" Friedrich Engels had written:

"Thus, full freedom in marriage can become generally operative only when the abolition of capitalist production, and of the property relations created by it, has removed all those secondary economic considerations which still exert so powerful an influence on the choice of a partner. Then, no other motive remains than mutual affection."

("The Origin of the Family, Private Property and the State," 1884, Marx and Engels, Selected Works in three volumes, Vol. 3, pp. 253-254)

Dharapani (Argakanchi) 1200 people came to the ANWA meting

Hari Acharya, parliamentary representative of the National People's Front, actively support the ANWA Campaign.

Karna giving a speech: here just a launch break was planned.

It is only possible to marry purely for love if no other considerations play a role be it the standing of the partner, his profession or be it how much money his family has and similar things. Here too we can see that, for example, with a divorce financial considerations often play a great role when people decide whether to leave their partner. In my opinion these constraints will only stop when financial dependence no longer exists. As Friedrich Engels said, this will only be possible in a society in which exploitation and oppression have been abolished.

In Nepal property rights for women are a step forward towards economic independence from their husbands. This right and the possibility to have their own job opens the way for women not to have to marry purely for reasons of financial support.

ANWA's Great Fight Against the "Dominance Problem"

Often when we talked about the concrete work of the ANWA women, we heard that they dealt with the "dominance problem". As we did not really know what they meant, we asked.

They described a real order of precedence in the families which is marked by tradition. A young woman who comes to the family of her husband is at the bottom of the family hierarchy. She is not only subordinate to her husbands and all male family members but also to the mother-in-law and the husband's sisters as long as they still live at home. The young wife often suffers harassment and also physical violence.

In several places the ANWA women told us that young women come to them because they have been beaten by their husband or are oppressed by their mother-in-law. The women are often completely at their mercy as they have no possibility to get out of this situation.

The ANWA representatives really tackle these two problems. They discuss it with the young woman and if she agrees the family is visited and they talk to the family members. Why do you hit your wives? Why do you pick on your daughters-in-law? They try to achieve solidarity but make it perfectly clear that they will make these incidents public if they continue in the future.

Here ANWA provides concrete personal aid. But this is only possible if the women do not see it as their private problem that they have to solve alone but dare to take the step and discuss it with other women and regard it as a common, social problem that they can solve.

ANWA does not leave the "dominance problem" to the courts which can only be found in large towns anyway but tackles the problem and tries to combat this form of oppression by convincing people that it is wrong and by using public pressure.

School books do support the ANWA women in their work against these traditions that discriminate against women. We find this out as guests of a family in Kohalpur.

Once again two children have given us their room so that we can spend the night there. In this family too, the father works in Saudi Arabia and only comes home on a rare visit. Through his work the family can afford to send their children to a private school, something that many families do if they can afford to.

At these private schools English is taught very early, in some schools as early as year three. For us this was very good because we were able to talk to the young people. Most of the women, however, could not speak English and we had to use gestures and sign language. In Kohalpur the son had to get his school bag from the room and he proudly showed us his school books. In his sociology book we happened to find the chapter on the family. There it said:

"Each family has someone at the head of the family who is responsible for running the family. The other members of the family obey the head of the family. The sense of oneness and love bind the members together."

In this way the feudal and bourgeois family structures are further anchored through the school books.

The Fight for Daily Life and the Liberation of Women - Two Sides of a Coin

At the daily meetings during the Campaign the ANWA women concentrated on the charter of women's rights and, in particular, on the demand for property rights. Because without economic independence from their husbands no equality is possible, is their argument.

(76)

In the many talks, usually before or after the big mass meetings, it became clear that in its painstaking daily work ANWA deals with a whole range of so-called everyday issues such as school attendance of girls, water supply in the mountain villages and also the daily issues caused by the state of emergency.

The women told us that in particular through the very close co-operation with the NPF, the NCP (Mashal) and also with other women's associations, parties and organisations their activities had really become mass Campaigns and could thus often be successfully organised.

It became very clear that in Nepal the women's movement does not cut itself off from other popular movements but, on the contrary, places great value on very close co-operation. For example, it went without saying that members of the NPF belonged to the Campaign team and spoke for the liberation of women from their point of view.

The NPF also actively supports women's liberation and gave vivid reports of the controversial discussions in parliament on the bills to grant women property rights. For them it is clear that the struggle for the liberation of women is not an isolated struggle but has to be conducted as part of the fight against overall exploitation and oppression. But they also criticise the conduct of men when necessary and appropriate.

They are, however, criticised for their active participation in the Campaign. In Butwal the representative of the women's organisation of the CPN (UML) said: "Why do you travel through the country with the women? You are members of parliament and your place is in parliament. It is there that decisions are made." But the NPF members of parliament said that for them it is much more important to encourage women to actively work for their interests, to prepare a position for themselves and not to rely on the parliament in Kathmandu. So often they had seen how bribery and influence had been used to pass laws in the interest of Indian industry. Also regarding provisions of the International Monetary Fund (IMF) on debt repayment, parliament does not have the possibility to decide in the interest of the people.

Girls do not Necessarily Attend School

We had hardly sat down in the Jeep in order to drive to the next meeting in Kapilvastu when it stopped and we looked at Laxmi questioningly. What's happening now? Nothing special to see far and wide.

Laxmi smiled at us and said: "Just a very small meeting. You only have to give a very small speech. Don't worry."

We gathered on the terrace of a house and a few chairs were quickly fetched, drinking water passed around and in no time at all 20 to 30 women had appeared. They had been waiting for us - but we did not know anything about it. Proudly the women of a Tharu village told us that together with ANWA they had fought for their children to be able to go to the state school.

It was above all the richer families who did not want the children from the Tharu village to also attend the state school. These are concrete effects of the caste system which contributes to the division of the population. But in the end the Tharu women got their way and their children, also the girls, can attend the school. They told us that they had to fight really hard for this. Now the women are fighting for their own right to attend school. Many of them cannot read or write. In this area there are no state-run programmes against illiteracy. Adults have no right to attend school. But they were confident that they would find a way to learn to read and write.

Although school attendance is compulsory in Nepal, nobody really checks whether children go to school or not; that is why many of the adults cannot read or write.

The fact that schools are often many hours' walk away and also poverty are reasons why children are not sent to school. It is not unusual that children, particularly the girls, have to work, either at home or outside and this is the reason that they do not attend school. In 1991 the illiteracy rate was still 55 percent, that of girls 75 percent.

In her letter to my daughter, Mira clearly describes how difficult it is for girls to get a good education.

Dear friend Sara, My name is Mira K.C. I read in class ten, I am 16 years old. I did sit my exam and I am preparing an S.L.C. examination. Dear friend I got your letter. In that letter your are requesting to make a pen friend. I also want to make you to my friend. In this letter I am going to write that my parents home, condition of my study and problems and conditions of Nepalese women. My parents home is Karnadhai and my father and mother occupation is farmer. In our country 80% people are in agriculture and uneducated. So that in our country farming is the main occupation of people. My father and mother work hard in the field to survive our life. I have one sister and one brother. My sister read in class six and my brother read in class seven in primary school.

I am going to write about my study. This is modern period and scientific period also. I think this is the most important thing in my life. But my condition is very poor. Being of my poor condition I can't get good education to my life. So that when I passed S.L.C. exam I should work hard to pay my campus. And I have to sweep and clean other house to pay copy, books and pen. In my students life there came many problems. Sometimes I didn't go to school because of my poor condition and I have to cut grass in my house. But my other rich friends didn't cut grass, they didn't work hard. So in my opinion I think that my student life is more miserable than other friends life.

Dear friend, I am going to write about conditions of Nepalese women. In our country there is big difference between men and women. Every part of employment there is a man. But women should not get chance to read. They should look after their children and cut grass in the house. And government should not care for women's problems. So that in our country women were sitting with their miserable life. Dear friend, I met your parents. Your parents know that condition of Nepalese women. If you ask your parents they tell you details of Nepalese women. At last I want to request you to visit Nepal. This much for this letter. See you again at our letter and photo.

Goodbye

The Fight Against Alcohol

In several places women told us that in recent years the alcohol consumption of some of the men had become a growing problem for the families. Unemployment drives the men to drink alcohol leading to serious problems in the families. "The little money they have is spent on the man's alcohol instead of on the family. The women no longer have any money to buy food for the children or go to the doctor if the children are ill," the women told us, some of them really angry.

I was actually surprised about this problem because in Nepal alcohol is by no means as socially accepted and normal as it is here. We were not offered alcohol at any party, celebration or visit during the whole Campaign. And sometimes somebody whispered to me about someone else: "He drinks alcohol."

The alcohol problem is a very new development in Nepal. In several travel guides or internet pages on Nepal I found the following sentence relating to economic support: "A beer factory was part of the German economic aid."

Durga Paudel told us how ANWA tackled the alcohol problem in the Pyuthan District and how they organised an anti-alcohol Campaign there: "We started at the lowest level, the wards. We invited the representatives of all the different parties because the problem concerns everyone. At the meeting we discussed in particular the harmful effects of alcohol and what consequences they have for the family.

Then we took our demands to the Place Development Committee and the District Development Committee. But we ANWA women were not satisfied with this. We went to the factory that makes the alcohol and made an ultimatum demanding that they stop alcohol production within 15 days. As they did not do this, of course, we went there after 15 days and poured the alcohol into the river. Of course, we could not solve the problem for ever by doing this. But what we achieved was that some Place Development Committees decided that anyone found drunk would have to pay a fine of 500 rupees."

The problem has, of course, not disappeared but ANWA has shown that they will fight for their cause and I can imagine that in Pyuthan there are many men who feel very uncomfortable if they get drunk and meet a group of ANWA women.

ANWA Fights for Water Supply in the Mountain Villages

Nepal is one of the countries with the most water in the world. With its many rivers which flow into the valleys from the mountains, neither water nor electricity supply should be a problem.

The hydroelectric potential is estimated today to be 83,000 megawatt meaning that Nepal could export electricity to India. But at the moment

(80)

Nepal can only cover one percent of its own electricity demand. In particular villages in the mountain regions often have no electricity and even in Kathmandu there are often power failures.

Water supply is equally bad. I am sure that many readers know the photos that show young girls who walk for many hours to get water and carry it home in jugs.

Amrita describes this problem in her letter to my daughter Sara: "We have many rivers but they are useless. The water from the rivers is used by the Indian government as Nepal's government is incapable of using the water."

Representatives of the NPF told us that the king of Nepal had sold the water rights to India and had thus made supply to Nepal's own population impossible. This makes them even more dependent on India.

In their fight for water supply ANWA always tries to explain the concrete reasons for the problems and thus win the people for a system without exploitation and oppression.

ANWA women from Okharkot told us that they have a serious problem with the government because they are demanding a good water supply: "In the past we had to walk more than two hours to get water for the family," they told us. Now they have a pipeline and tank that supplies them with water. "That is progress if it works," they went on. But the water supply is very irregular and sometimes they only get water from the pipeline every other day.

The government says the problems lie in the fact that three valleys are supplied via this pipeline and they happen to be the last valley so that there is not always enough water.

But the women do not accept this explanation. They do not give up and demand a permanent water supply from the government. With this demand they unite all the women, and also men from this valley.

What We Need are Jobs

We were standing on the Okharkot, a mountain peak with the ruins of an old fortress, a small temple and a magnificent view over three valleys.

Right at the top of a tree a Red Flag had been hanging from a bamboo cane for many years. In this area not many people are interested in removing the flag because it is a stronghold of the NCP (Mashal). And the few who would like to remove it do not dare to because on a wooden board it says the following:

"If this red flag is removed, a bomb will explode. But if it does not explode a curse will befall the perpetrator."

To our great surprise 650 people attended a mass meeting here. The participants came here on foot from three different valleys and every time we wondered: Where do these people come from? How long did it take them to walk here to attend the meeting? How deep must their solidarity with this movement be that they go to so much trouble?

As we had been on this peak since sunrise and were enjoying the fine weather, the calm and the wonderful view, we could see the people gradually coming up the mountain. We also had the time to talk to a few women. So with the help of our patient interpreter I asked the women who had just-arrived: "What is your greatest wish? What should change first?"

"We need jobs in Nepal, we want our husbands to be able to work here. Look at this village; it's Bangie. Here 90 percent of the men work abroad and this is Okharkot. Here it is over 50 percent but the husbands are only able to send money irregularly. And here in the third village it is no different. Here we don't know the exact figures. "

They told us that very many men work in India and also in Saudi Arabia, the United Arab Emirates, Malaysia and other countries. Demands for a national economy, against further privatisation of the industry that still exists and, above all, against the sell-out of the country's resources, were discussed by the women.

Dependence on India and also on Germany and the USA were seen as the main reasons for the lack of development of their own industry.

Labour emigration means a life without a family and the women have to organise their whole lives alone. As the men can only send back very little money, the women have to feed the whole family by farming a smallholding, usually with their parents-in-law, and have to ensure their own livelihoods. Despite the problems that this development causes, it has a new and important side. There is much more self-confidence among the women who see that they are able to master their own lives. As they are responsible for everything, they leave the confines of the household.

(82)

This leads to them think more about the social causes of their situation, to organise themselves and thus create the foundations for their struggle for liberation.

But the women did admit to us that some of their husbands are not so happy about their new self-confidence. The husbands have to do away with the old, traditional ideas and accept that they are no longer the masters in the house. Some of them try to forbid their wives from attending the meetings. But after having met the ANWA women, I know that these men will not be very successful with their attitudes.

Great Self-confidence of the Women and the Issue of Children

One of the nicest small discussion groups was in Shandhi Kharka, the district capital of Argha Khanchi. It was organised because I had kept asking to be able to talk to the women more directly and exchange opinions. This was not easy because the Campaign tour had a very tight schedule and almost every day we went one to another place. It took hours to travel just 20 kilometres on the difficult roads.

About 50 women came to this meeting and some of them had walked for several days to be here. After they had asked lots and lots of questions about women in Germany, how we live, how many children we have etc., I was able to ask my questions about their living conditions and their ANWA work.

Suddenly there was an almost awkward atmosphere in the room and nobody really dared to say anything until one woman finally plucked up courage and started.

She apologised, as many women in other places had also done, for not being modern and educated and that for this reason she could not express her feelings and speak.

It was as if they had been indoctrinated to believe that women are really not able to conduct their own fight for liberation. I had a completely different opinion. A women's association which despite a state of emergency, is able to organise a Campaign of this sort in which, despite a ban and so much work at home, thousands of women find the courage and time to attend meetings, to represent their interests, is able to change something. These women are educated. Above all they really know how to take charge of their concerns themselves and they are progressive!

This argument almost had the effect of liberation and the women told us how they organise their work. For example, two women were going to be arrested because they collected donations for this Campaign. They kicked up such a fuss at the police that they were immediately released.

They mentioned a lot of old-fashioned traditions which they had to fight to participate in ANWA's work.

The husband did not want the wife to attend meetings.

The mother-in-law was against girls attending school.

Having a lot of children is part of the good reputation of a family.

Usually the women found a way to solve the problems together. The issues were discussed in the families with a group of women.

Proudly and also roguishly they told us that in this village no family has more than four children. This, they said, is the result of the intensive discussions of the ANWA women in the families. They had to overcome several obstacles:

• Tradition does not allow a woman to reject a man; most women do not want to accept the suggestion of one women simply not to get married;

• Hinduism does not allow any family planning because children are a gift from God;

• And tradition says that a husband has the right to take more wives if his wife does not give birth to a son.

Under these conditions a successful family planning programme demands a lot of courage and conscientiousness from the women. The women realise that having a lot of children only increases their poverty and stops them from being active. So they have managed to limit the number of children per family to a maximum of four.

They are below the usual average birth rate per woman in Nepal which in 1991 was 5.6 children and in 1999 4.3. But in rural areas, which definitely includes their village, the rate is much higher than this average. In comparison: In Germany the average number of children is 1.3.

In Nepal too, it can be seen that particularly in the towns families are getting smaller and the birth rate is falling drastically.

We Have a Lot in Common...

When we arrived in Kathmandu I had given the then President of ANWA, Durga Paudel, one of the folders with the letters from German women as a present. She loved the letters and immediately said she would have the letters translated into Nepalese. We were very glad but had not yet understood the significance of the letters. Two weeks later the Campaign team received a parcel with 1000 brochures. They had really translated all the letters and had them printed. The brochures met with such great interest that by the end of the Campaign all of the 1000 brochures had been sold.

In her thank you letter to the German women in the brochure Durga Paudel writes.[7]

What Made these Letters so Interesting for the Women in Nepal ?

We were often asked if and why there is a women's movement in Germany? They said women have legal equality and come from one of the richest countries in the world. Why do women in Germany still fight for their liberation?

It is, of course, true that we come from one of the richest countries in the world. But are workers in Germany really rich? Aren't the majority of women in Germany exploited and oppressed?

The women in Nepal had not known that there is great unemployment in Germany and that also over four million women have jobs where they have practically no protection rights. It was also new to them that most women in Germany go through a daily ordeal.

With the help of the letters we were able to explain that in comparison it is, without doubt, a lot of money that Margit, for example, earns as a factory worker. But that people in Germany have to pay around 500 to 600• for a 3 to 4 room flat was unthinkable.

_____

7. The reply of ANWA to women of Germany is given in Appendix-B, page 129.

That many people have a car not as a luxury but simply need it to get to work.

That people in Germany generally do not have a garden for the purpose of growing the food they need and many more things.

If we were to make a journey like this again, we would take a large folder with pictures of our daily lives. What a kitchen looks like, a cooker, a school etc. There was an almost unquenchable interest in the lives of the people and also in the problems and perspectives confronting people in Germany.

At meetings I increasingly read out letters from women in Germany to explain the position of women in Germany and to present the central demands of the German women's movement. By referring to the lives of the women who wrote the letters I was able to explain that in Germany too, in a technically highly developed country, women still have to fight for an equal position in society.

The way was now free to seek the reasons for the oppression and exploitation of women in both countries and also to seek a solution together.

Discussion no longer focussed on what divided us in our lives but the search for common ground and common interests so that we can work together.

One of the main problems of the women in Nepal, they said, is that they are tied to the house, they have to run the whole household, raise the children, look after the animals, cultivate the small piece of land in front of the house, so that they have hardly any time to be active.

Their day usually starts at 5 a.m. and generally they do not finish their daily chores until late in the evening. It is not unusual for women to work 16 hours a day.

We were able to show that many women in Germany have the same number of tasks to do and that they have to bear the responsibility for the whole family. Although most of them have jobs outside the house they are still responsible for everything. They have to cope with a permanent balancing act of managing both a job and a family with the result that there is never enough time for either.

So for women in Germany one of the main issues is also: Do I fight for the time to be active?

We also saw that in both countries the responsibility of women for home and family is organised by a large number of customs, moral ideas and traditions. Just as in Germany, Nepalese women have the moral duty of being responsible for the children.

The idea that a woman might leave her husband because she does not love him was almost impossible for them to imagine. In Nepal a woman always has to stand faithfully by her man. In Germany this is no longer the case in this sense. But we have all heard people saying things like: "Divorce is out of the question. Just think of the children."

And last but not least, some of the things we have in common are that women have to be persuaded to develop their self-confidence, that we do understand politics and are able to conduct the fight for women's liberation. We agreed that statements such as: "We women in Nepal are backward and uneducated, " are just as untrue as the opinion of many German women: "1 don't understand politics."

Often enough it is women who prove what abilities they have. But they are the last to see this.

When we looked for the reasons for this we both struck gold.

In their Charter of Women's Rights ANWA writes:

"Overhauling the present family system is one of the pre-requisites for the liberation of Women. It is this family structure which confines the women to household works and prevents them from expressing their feelings against the discrimination in the name of gender."

In my faithful reference book "New Perspectives for the Liberation of Women" I looked to see what I could find on the origins of the special oppression of women. On page 66 I found what I was looking for. There Lenin is quoted, a quotation that really impresses me, especially the last part of the sentence. It appeared in many of the speeches I gave in Nepal.

Lenin wrote this on the occasion of International Women's Day.

"For under capitalism the female half of the human race is doubly oppressed. The working woman and the peasant women are oppressed by capital, but over and above that, even in the most democratic of the bourgeois republics, they remain, firstly, deprived of some rights because the law does not give them equality with men; and secondly - and this is

(87)

the main thing - they remain in "household bondage"..., for they are overburdened with the drudgery of the most squalid, backbreaking and stultifying toil in the kitchen and the family household." (Lenin. International Women's Day, Collected Works, Vol. 32, p. 161)

The conclusions drawn by the authors on the same page:

"In the responsibility of women for private housekeeping and family affairs management lies the material foundation for the double oppression of the masses of women in capitalism. This double oppression far from occurs primarily in the form of open use of force by men against women." (p. 66) The functions of the production and reproduction of human life are of such nature that they cannot be upheld for long through open violence, by laws, decrees or threats of punishment. It is the purpose of the bourgeois world outlook, and particularly of tradition and morality, to make the role of the woman in this appear natural, ordained by God, and inconceivable in any other form. "(p. 73)

Our discussions on the reasons for the particular oppression of women intensified this idea more and more and I often included it in my small speeches. We realised that for society to exist without exploitation and oppression, family structures have to be overcome which bind women to the household and which make the responsibility for the children a private task of the family instead of making it a task of society as a whole.

ANWA - a Women's Association with Mass Influence

Nepal is one of the poorest countries in the world with the eleventh largest rate of illiteracy in the world and with traditions which discriminate against women that we can hardly imagine. Who would ever have thought that such a country could have such a strong liberation movement and, above all, such a strong women's movement?

Here we are often given the impression that people can only suffer under such miserable conditions, that they have no strength to liberate themselves, that they just vegetate and need our sympathy and leadership. We are told they depend on the help of western specialists and so-called "development aid".

(88)

This women's movement is proof that this picture is wrong and that we can learn a lot from this strength, determination, perseverance and awareness.

State of Emergency no Deterrent

The Campaign had been planned by the women for over a year and then in November 2001 the state of emergency was declared.

This, of course, led to many discussions among the women: Can we continue our Campaign despite this? Isn't it too dangerous? Can we accept responsibility for the security of the foreign delegations? Will we get through the military checks?

"There are no difficult conditions under which we cannot fight, we just have to take these conditions into account."

This was the decisive argument which led to the continuation of the Campaign.

ANWA knew, of course, that they were not alone in organising the Campaign. Above all, ANWA was able to count on the many members and supporters in the country. It was them who mobilised people for the Campaign, who organised beds for the Campaigners, cooked food for the team and much more. Often women had to walk for days to attend meetings. How could arrangements be made if there is no telephone? If none of the women have a car to drive to the next village? And bus and road connections do not exist everywhere. And last but not least, for many ANWA women attendance at meetings or the time needed for organising the work means real loss of or less income.

I was really shocked to hear of Tulsipur's experience. At a small meeting of about 50 to 60 women we passionately discussed the fight for property rights and the different experiences in the struggle for the liberation of women. A charming, somewhat elderly lady also keenly discussed this matter. At the end she spoke again. She told us that she is an ANWA woman with her whole heart, that she was really happy to be there today and that she would not have missed the meeting for anything. But she had one problem:

"I attended the meeting and that was good but now I have not cut the grass for the buffalo. Without grass the buffalo won't give any milk, without milk not enough food for the children."

No solution could be found for this woman because many women who attended this meeting or other meetings had exactly the same problem.

But it clearly shows what it means for the women to be active. It does not only demand a great willingness to make sacrifices but also awareness that this is the only right and consistent fight, the only way to overcome poverty and oppression.

When I look through my diary I have to say that there was really not one day on which no meeting was held. Although Laxmi sometimes came to me and said: "Gabi, today you don't have to give any talks, there's no meeting planned, today you can have a rest", it never actually was like that because the ANWA women always found reasons to hold small meetings that had not been planned.

Corner Meetings

After two to three hours in the Jeep with seventeen people and beautiful sunshine, a break is sometimes necessary. So out of the Jeep, into the tea house. But why should we just drink tea?

An ANWA women always had the idea to quickly hold a corner meeting. Without us noticing, a member of the Campaign team went through the street with the megaphone and called a small meeting. "Drink up your tea, it's starting," called Mina and quickly put a table to which the ANWA poster was fixed into the street. The megaphone was already there. That's all the ANWA women needed. They knew what to say, they did not need written texts and they really inspired the people. None of these corner meetings were attended by fewer than 100 people. Sometimes 20 to 30 brochures were also sold, either the letters from the women in Germany or their own brochures on the work of ANWA.

In the Evening Before we Went to Bed

We really only wanted to sleep there but when the women heard that we were there they came from the neighbourhood to welcome us. And suddenly fifty women were sitting there and there were proper little meetings. "Tell the women something now that they are here..."

"But only if they tell us something about themselves."

Here Just a Meal was Planned

The Pyuthan district was behind us and we were on our way to Karhadhai. As in Nepal people eat the first meal between 10 and 11 a.m., at this time of day a family was always visited who was responsible for the team's food that day. Today Karna's family was responsible for the food. We already knew Karna from the first weeks and we were looking forward to seeing him again. In the first week he had been involved in preparing the Campaign and during the preparation period he was stopped by a military control and beaten up. With a burst eardrum and a damaged kidney he was helped onto the stage in Dhangarhi where he held a stirring speech against the state of emergency and for women's rights to property. Only after this did he drive on with us in the Jeep and was taken to hospital.

We should have known. Karna would insist on welcoming the Campaign team with a big meeting. We got out of the Jeep, were showered with garlands of flowers, had to shake numerous hands and at a meeting attended by over 300 people the ANWA women talked about their Campaign. I was able to talk about the lives of women in Germany, about the women's movement in Germany and about the many common experiences which we had already made in recent weeks.

An ANWA Activist Introduces Herself

Dear Women in Germany,

My name is Nirmala Aryal and I have two sisters and two brothers. I am 39 years old. My mother and father are dead. I got married twenty years ago; 1 was 19 years old. My husband is 41. My parents said at the time that I should marry him; today I am very happy. My parents organised this marriage. Love came in the course of the marriage. Before I did not love my husband. I did not know him before. My father picked him. My parents did not have to give a dowry.

Now I live here with my daughter and two sons. We have a rice mill and I am active in ANWA. I am on the district committee. I attended school for ten years. Four years ago we came here. My husband and I are workers. We used to live in India. In India my husband worked at the Iron and Steel Company. All five of us (we have three children) lived in India during this time. The children were all born there and went to school there, too. In India we were also both politically active. My husband was on the central committee of the All India Nepalese Unity Society I worked for ANWA and was the President of the Association of Nepalese Women in India.

My parents-in-law do not live here. My husband and I came back here and we built up a small rice factory. During the rice season 20 workers work at our factory, otherwise just 3 to 4. They live here. When it is not the season the workers return to their houses.

Here I have been working for ANWA for one year. The women here have many problems. One problem is that men hit their wives. They also have economic problems. The men drink wine and then they hit their wives. There are also great problems with the children because the children are often ill. But there is no doctor here and they have no money for medicine. The men need the money to drink wine and do not spend it one the children for them to go to the doctor. They consume what they own to drink wine and then there is no money for the family. That is the main problem.

I go to these women and we discuss how we can solve the problems. It is not easy for the women to leave their husbands because they do not have any property rights. They try to talk to their husbands but often they do not listen. There is very little success. In a few cases they can solve the problems but not usually.

The District Committee has seven members. We are just starting the work here. It is progressing very slowly. As I have to work at the rice factory I only have very little time for the ANWA work.

My wish is that ANWA will grow really big. We have no full-timers here so it is difficult to develop the work. In India I worked more for ANWA. It is not easy because I work more at our small factory than if I worked somewhere else. We had to build up this small business in order to give our children an education. But I would like to do more at ANWA.

It is nice to see that the German women also fight for their liberation. I wish that women would help each other. The friendship between the women in Nepal and Germany should grow. Our standards of living are different. The demand for property rights is new for us but in Germany it is no problem. For us it is a major demand. For us it is very important that we get equal rights. We will fight for them in parliament.

My wish is that women from Germany help us because the women there are educated, but not here. The women could help us in the education and training of the women. We could exchange new ideas on solving problems. The fact that you are here gives the women courage and they are very happy. New members become more active and are mobilised because other organisations notice that ANWA has contacts with Germany; some are sad that they do not have this contact.

We are very happy that you are visiting us and we hope that these visits will be repeated from time to time. This could help ANWA. Our women will become more active through this, they will gain courage and become more open.

We need a common language to discuss the social problems. I would really love to have a deep talk with you and exchange ideas but we do not have a common language.

Best wishes

Nirmala

We grew really fond of Nirmala during the Campaign. On the very first day of our journey, before we had even reached the Campaign team, we were invited to eat at her house. She watched us inquisitively and we felt her frustration because she wanted to ask questions but could not speak English. The interview with her was held one week later. Here she said that she had little time for the ANWA work, that she wanted help from the women from Germany. We said goodbye a second time. Shortly afterwards to our great surprise we suddenly saw Nirmala appear again. First she followed us by bus to take part in the Campaign wherever possible. Some days later she was there with her bag. She participated in the Campaign for over a week, travelled with us in the Jeep and developed into an enthusiastic speaker. We did not notice that she was uneducated, like she said she was. It was clear that a self-confident woman was speaking who knew why she is fighting and what she wants. It became really lively. International solidarity in the women's movement is not a one way street. What is important is mutual support and mutual learning.

The Success Team of Dharapani

It was not easy to get to these women who, through their systematic work, were responsible for organising in their village the biggest meeting with 1200 people.

There is just one street to Shandhi Kharka to the district capital, if this path can even be called a street. And on this journey it started to rain. The first still "harmless" step was: stop, get all the luggage into the Jeep with the 17 people and carry on. Comfort, if there ever was any, was now over.

In no time the clay track was completely muddy and it was impossible to carry on. Luckily at the top of the hill there was a small tea house where we could wait till the rain stopped. But how were we to carry on? After a short discussion it was clear that it was impossible to carry on in the Jeep. The Jeep could only drive on when the road was dry. Later we heard that during the rainy season the whole district is cut off from the outside world for two months.

As it was unclear when the Jeep would be able to follow us we had to decide quickly what luggage we would need for the next couple of days. I took a toothbrush, clean underwear and the laptop. My husband had similar priorities and decided to take his camera equipment. So we started walking to Shandhi Kharka.

It was just turning dark when we reached the first houses. Dilaram, the NPF member of parliament, who was accompanying us, started making lots of phone calls. We did not understand what it was all about. Can't we just carry on before it gets dark? What do the phone calls mean? After an hour we were told to carry on.

What had happened? Dilaram had been making phone calls until he received permission from the local chief of police that we could walk into the town in the dark and was assured that the police had been instructed not to shoot. Once again we had completely underestimated the effects of the state of emergency.

But now to our women from Dharapani where we arrived three days later. The place is located one valley further on. We were completely baffled how in such an isolated place 1200 people could come to an ANWA meeting, at least 80 percent of whom were women. Where do

Kapilvastu District: army burns down a village

Kanchanpur District: army uses elephants to trample down a village by night

Kumi Shera (Baglung): a minute's silence in memory of the victims of the state of emergency.

Canvassing at a corner meeting.

these people live we kept asking ourselves. There always just seemed to be a few groups of houses as far as we could see.

Dilaram was Proud to present to us the ANWA district committee. This is his constituency. One woman is a teacher, all the others are farmers.

We really wanted to know what their secret is: how do they mobilise so many women?

It turned out that this committee does very intensive work. They go from house to house and promote the meetings and the work of ANWA. In this place they meet once a week to discuss all sorts of issues. They use any opportunity to talk to the neighbours, be it at the well when they fetch water or do the washing. Wherever the women are, they are there too.

They said that there is nothing that is not discussed. They talk about everything that interests them and affects their lives. This includes socialism they proudly told us. They do not restrict themselves to women's issues. Everything is discussed. As social problems are not easy to understand and the women have a lot of questions, they sometimes organise courses. If possible they receive support from the ANWA Central Committee or from representatives of the NCP (Mashal).

Unfortunately at 5 p.m. we had to stop because we had to be in our sleeping quarters before nightfall.

We finished this tour on foot too. This time the axle of a tractor had broken and the road was blocked. Taking along the same sort of things as three days before we walked back to Shandhi Kharka in the hope that the Jeep would arrive by the next day so that we could continue our Campaign tour.

Women's Property Rights - A Controversial Subject in Nepal

With the idea that nobody could really have anything against property and divorce rights for women I attended the first press conference. But here my eyes were opened.

Some journalists, who were still quite young, were openly critical of the Campaign.

They said that if women had the right to get divorced, they would get divorced every few years and marry another man. The whole family system would break down.

They had similar arguments regarding property rights. Property rights for women, they said, would destroy and overturn Nepal's whole social order. How could ANWA representatives ever imagine anything like this?

My answer here would certainly have been short and precise, something like: "If social order does not grant women these elementary rights, then it is not worth existing. "I am sure this would have led to very controversial discussions.

Later the ANWA women told me that by no means all women's associations make these demands and that there are some differences of opinion between the associations. For example, the women's association of the Nepalese Congress Party, the ruling reactionary party, only demands for women the right to education and the right to work. On the issues of property and divorce rights these women argue in a similar way to the journalists.

ANWA Does not Like Non-Governmental Organisations (NGOs)

At the third or fourth meeting the local ANWA women in Manakaman started talking about the NGOs. They asked: "Are there also so many NGOs in Germany and do they also make so many problems for you? They are a real counter--movement against the independently organised women's fight for their liberation."

Of course I was aware of the arguments about the work of the NGOs. In Germany too there are lots of women's organisations who regard themselves as NGOs. Mostly these organisations focus their work on lobbying. I was keen to hear what the women would tell me. At the same time I looked up to see what my book on women's issues said. There I found:

"Since the imperialist-dominated UN has no interest in the development of a militant women's movement, petty-bourgeois feminism

Market street in the district capital of Baglung.

Laxmi's family: the mother had four daughters, the husband took a second wife.

Class in a state school.

On the way to Pyuthan

was systematically injected into the international women's movement through the UN and especially so-called non-governmental organizations (NGOs), and has become an element of neo--colonialist rule. "

An important effect of the women's policy of these NGOs is the division between men and women and between women's movement and revolutionary movement. The Marxist-Leninist Kathy Nadkar from India tells about this:

"There were many discussions about the women question, mainly under the influence of non-governmental organizations, which treated the contradiction between man and woman as antagonistic. They attempt to undermine the role of the party. As excuse they use the argument that the Left neglects the women's issue. The NGOs launched a Campaign which was financed from abroad. The result was that many previously active women were moved to passivity or now work in NGOs. They received academic training and were pulled out of the militant women's movement and the Marxist-Leninist movement. " (Conversation of April 28, 1998 with Monika Gartner-Engel).

This hits the nail on the head as far as the women in Nepal are concerned. The ANWA women told me, for example, that in some districts there are a large number of mothers' group who are closely linked to the National Democratic Party but who deliberately call themselves NGO. These mothers' groups work primarily at a local level and always deal with one concrete project be it hygienic conditions, self-organised reading and writing programmes and much more, things that are really very sensible. The ANWA women told us that at first they had also worked in these mothers' groups. But disagreements soon occurred because our ANWA women also wanted the groups to discuss the reasons for the problems, how women can do more than social work and also become politically active. The official representatives of these mothers' groups was against this. They said they received funding to organise social services and they did not want political discussions in these groups. The ANWA women decided to stop any more co--operation with these groups.

ANWA criticises that the people are left in the dark regarding the reasons for poverty in Nepal. Usually they are told that it is due to their lack of education and the underdeveloped state of the country. Thus the people themselves are given the blame for the state of the country.

(101)

They also told us that some NGOs pay women so-called meeting money amounting to 50 to 100 rupees, which amounts to the daily wages of a peasant, and that they had lost many members through this work. The NGOs usually have money to organise certain projects and promise the women work, some women really getting work. ANWA, on the other hand, has no money to distribute; on the contrary, they regularly collect donations for their own work and to be a member of ANWA costs 20 rupees a year.

And this is the fierce argument among the women. Should we be dependent on outside aid, be told by other, usually foreign, representatives what is right and wrong for us and our country or should we go our own way, use our own heads, recognise the causes of the problems in our country and strive for a society without exploitation and oppression?

In the Baglung District, where we visited a relative of a member of our Campaign team, there happened to be a "women's meeting" of a Danish NGO. Our hostess worked for this NGO. The group was just being visited by representatives who were presenting a "small credit programme" for women. We had the impression that this was some sort of chain letter system. The women were to start with a deposit of 150 dollars and were to find more women interested in this project. Later, if enough women took part in this scheme, they would get back a much larger sum.

The full-time employee was also very skeptical about this idea but was not able to convince the women of the dangers of this project. We kept asking questions because the whole thing made a very dubious impression on us. But unfortunately the three women soon left with their bright folders. So we did not find out exactly what the women were being offered. As I considered discussion about the NGOs to be very important, I mentioned the subject in a talk with members of the ANWA Central Committee.

They told me that as far as they know there are over 6000 such NGOs in Nepal. In a press article from nepalnews.com from the year 2000, they mentioned that there were 15,000 NGOs and "welfare groups". This incredible number made me investigate why there are so many NGOs. I could not really understand it. The reason though is that NGOs do not have to pay any tax or produce invoices. In an internet article it says:

"Although a very large number of organisations and people try to help, most of the Nepalese organisations at least are private companies and only enrich families or interest groups. Thus it is estimated that less than 10 percent of the money actually helps those for whom it is intended. If the sums that come into the country are added up, it is no surprise that nothing changes."

(www.navyonepal.com/politicsviluppo d.htm)

ANWA now has a very rigorous attitude to NGOs and INGOs (INGOs are organisations that work with money from abroad, for example the Friedrich-Ebert Foundation which is represented in Nepal with many projects). They say that anybody who is a member of an NGO cannot become a member of ANWA. They said that they plan a Campaign against the harmful effect of the NGOS. "Because if we do nothing against them influencing the women we will lose a large number of members to these organisations, "said the ANWA representatives. The main arguments of the NGOs against the political organisation of women are:

• They claim to be independent, they say that we do not need any parties and political organisations. In reality they make the women dependent on foundations, organisations and financial backers.

• The NGOs say a revolutionary movement, is not necessary, the women can achieve their aims through parliamentary channels, especially in the struggle against men. In reality they are tying the women to an outdated system which strengthens the oppression and exploitation of the people even more.

• The NGOs say the solution to the women's problems depends on their education. If the women were educated they would be much better off. In reality the problem of the women is the dependence of their country on India or the imperialist countries such as Germany and the USA which prevent the country from developing its own economy thus increasing poverty among the population.

In this way the NGOs contribute to the division between women and men and also to a separation between women's and liberation movements. They also consistently work against the independent political organisation of women in Nepal for their liberation.

In this field in particular I wish ANWA much success in their work against the undermining effect of these organisations on the struggle of the women's movement in Nepal.

A Great Wish for Unity in the Struggle for Liberation of Women

During the All Nepalese Women's Campaign ANWA considered co-operation with other groups and parties to be very important because it is essential that all groups work together in the issue of property rights for women, against laws that discriminate against women, for the liberation of women. Unity is absolutely essential.

The so called interaction meetings, which were usually held in towns, served this purpose.

It was not unusual for representatives from up to ten different groups and parties to speak at these meetings. They all expressed their deep respect for ANWA because ANWA has not been deterred by the state of emergency. In Kapilvastu I was most impressed by the representative of the Nepalese Congress Party. She congratulated the ANWA speaker Durga Paudel on her excellent speech on women's rights. She said she could subscribe to every word that Durga had said. She thus openly opposed the demands of her own party which rejects women's right to property and divorce.

She instantly said she would translate Durga's speech into the language of the women of the area because she thought that many of the women had not understood Durga's speech and she felt they should. She invited Durga to come to this district again for a week or two so that they could conduct a small Campaign here together.

All these interaction meetings were attended by members of parties such as the CPN (UML) or other women's organisations.

Apart from the good luck wishes that ANWA received, the wish was always expressed that they should conduct their struggle together. It became clear that they need an organisation which brings together the different forces of the women's movement in Nepal. The representatives of the Central Committee were of the opinion that they had to consider what they could do about the wish for joint action, to consider how it can be possible to work together beyond party lines.

We are familiar with the wish for greater unity in the women's movement from Germany and at the meeting I talked about our experience in organising the Women's Political Counsel which Durga Paudel had attended in Germany in the year 2000.

The Women's Political Counsel is a forum of an equal exchange of opinion and experience in the fighting women's movement. It does not represent competition to existing organisations but offers a platform for all currents in the women's movement (with the exception of fascist organisations) to present their work, to talk to participants and to look at and discuss new ideas and experiences. Thus a major step towards greater unity, clear objectives and determination in the fighting women's movement.

In my speech in Tansen I presented the major principles of the Women's Political Counsel organised on a non-partisan basis and was eager to hear what the women in Nepal would say. I summarised it as follows:

We need co-operation with the following guidelines:

• We are a non-partisan forum of equal exchange of opinion and experience and consider ourselves to be part of a fighting, international women's movement.

• We must not cut ourselves off from other movements and need special solidarity with the workers' movement.

• We practice objective debate in solidarity

• We work as equals on the basis of ideological openness

• We finance our work jointly, independently and autonomously.

To my surprise the principles caused fierce discussion at this meeting. Some speakers welcomed the principles and emphasised the wish for closer co--operation among women. Others criticised the split in the women's movement in Nepal. Partisan women's organisations prevented the unity of the women's movement. This was particularly criticised by some teachers or journalists. Then the representative of the National Democratic Party started to speak. He welcomed the principles and was of the opinion that it was important that women organise. themselves outside political parties. He quoted the example of the mothers' groups, which I described earlier on, and said that here women united independently of political parties and, he said, this was the way the position the German colleague supported. "Stop, "I thought, "now it's getting difficult because this is really not my opinion." Non-partisan does not mean that party representatives are excluded but that they co-operate as equals. Quickly Dilaram, the representative of the NPF, with whom I had often discussed the non-partisan character of the Women's Political Counsel and the women's association Courage, came to my aid. He was very interested in why there are these non-partisan forms of organisation in Germany. He answered for me and explained the principle of non-partisanship: "Here women with different ideologies who support different parties work together as equals."

On other occasions we discussed the importance of the different principles. I was asked what significance the guideline of ideological openness had, whether this was not something normal. I told them that in Germany anti-communism is very strong and that for this reason for many groups it is not normal, for example, to organise a joint Campaign on International Women's Day, with Marxist-Leninists for example. Our ANWA women were surprised about the anti-communism. I was frequently asked why there is this anti-communism in Germany and this often led to interesting discussions on our and their history.

It was very interesting for me to learn that for people in Nepal it is normal to co-operate with Marxist-Leninists. Socialism is well established among the population. As there are several different Marxist-Leninist parties in Nepal, we were asked again and again what directions we thought were good and correct. The people automatically thought that we consider Marxism-Leninism right, at least we were never asked what we think about this subject.

The Nepalese are like Thomas Mann who described anti-communism as "the greatest folly of the 20th century."

It is a great success of ANWA that at their meetings they managed to bring together representatives of different directions irrespective of party barriers. This is a major precondition for continuing to unite women on a fighting basis for the struggle for their rights

Klara Zetkin at the International Women's Day in Nepal

8 March, International Women's Day, fell right in the middle of the Campaign and so we were able to celebrate it in Nepal. Our Nepalese friends were sad that we were unable to hold this event outside in Tulsipur but that we had to use a hall. A public demonstrations was not allowed during the state of emergency.

On this day Mina held the main speech for ANWA. I was more than a little surprised when my translator suddenly spoke about Klara Zetkin. Mina praised Klara Zetkin as a great representative of the German women's movement who before and during the Weimar Republic actively fought for the liberation of women with the newspaper "Gleichheit". First Klara Zetkin was a member of the SPD but changed later to the KPD (Communist Party of Germany) because she said she "wanted to fight where life is". Here in Nepal this important German woman is remembered on International Women's Day; and ANWA was particularly proud to now have here a representative of the women's movement from this country.

It was, of course, clear that I had to rewrite my speech a little because I had to at least talk a little about Klara Zetkin and the history of 8 March. In this situation I realised how good the courses and educational work organised by the ANWA activists must be if they are so familiar with the history of the international women's movement. This made me curious to learn more about their courses and educational work.

Our ANWA women confirmed that they hold regular courses. As the women's association of the NCP (Mashal) it is normal that they organise courses on the principles of Marxism-Leninism. They also deal with the theory of the struggle of women and that is why they were familiar with the name Klara Zetkin.

In the villages and districts the ANWA women organise courses with the groups dealing with topical issues and problems of the women.

I thought of the ANWA office - no computer or typewriter, with very few books - I thought of the bad roads and bus connections, the long marches to get to the women in the villages.

It is such an achievement of the ANWA activists to build up and run this women's association under these conditions! My respect for and solidarity with these women grew from day to day.

Learning from the History of the International Women's Movement

"Oh, by the way, in three days there's a seminar in Butwal. If you want to you can prepare a talk on the Charter of Women's Rights and the international women's movement. That would be very nice. It will definitely be interesting and we are curious to hear what you have to say." With this information I heard about the seminar and was looking forward to see what awaited me. But first the story of the little slips of paper.

The little slips of paper

I really liked the little slips of paper. We all know the situation. You are at a meeting and still feel a bit unsure but you have so many questions. But what can you do? There are 10 to 200 people sitting here whom I do not know. Will they laugh at me when I ask my question? Can I formulate it correctly? Questions like this really trouble people and because of this some important things are not said or questions not asked. No problem at the ANWA meetings in Nepal. Here little notes were passed to the platform. Women who did not want to talk or ask questions personally, simply wrote on little slips of paper. They were taken to the representative to whom the question was addressed. Like this no question, no thought was lost. A good idea that t was happy to take home with me.

But now back to the seminar in Butwal. For this seminar a seminar paper had been prepared[8] that had already been sent to the different representatives of other groups and organisations. At the seminar it was presented for discussion. This was unfortunately a very difficult task for our translator and we did not understand everything said in this discussion. But the seminar paper, that was translated into English for me and which I was able to read later, was very interesting. I was surprised at the detailed presentation of the history of the women's movement in Europe which had obviously been intensively studied in order to learn from it.

I take a twelve-hour flight to one of the poorest countries in the world about which I knew hardly anything before, very little about the lives of the people and even less about the history. There I meet people who have dealt intensively with the European history of the women's movement to learn about the transition from feudalism to capitalism for their own liberation movement. I would like to present readers a few excerpts:

"In the wake of revolution against feudalism , people started raising their voices against all sort of injustice with a view to raising their economic political and social status. In Renaissance period of Europe,

---

8. *The paper was prepared by Com. M.B. Singh, General Secretary of the Nepal Communist Party (Mashal). Full text of the paper is given in Appendix -E, (Page 154)*

(108)

women raised their voice against feudal, traditional and outdated values thereby showing their awareness for the freedom of themselves from the discriminatory tradition and social system. After the industrial revolution, there was a wave of bourgeoisie democratic revolution throughout Europe. Together with it they started to take more initiative for their rights and began to form unions for the struggle for their rights. During feudalism women were confined to household work. But capitalism brought a large number of the women out of their kitchens. Women then began to go to the market and find jobs like men. This helped the women work in the factory together with the men.. They also started working in different offices. This was a great contribution made by capitalism for the liberation movement of women. ...

"In our country Nepal too along with the gradual introduction of capitalist economy, the process of women coming out of house, has started. Women have now begun to work in the offices, industries and factories. They are no more confined to the narrow domestic walls. The changes in the fields of society and economic helped women to achieve more rights, although it is a partial progress. The changes of this type have also inspired them to fight for their freedom and in last a few decades there have been significant changes in progressive way."

I thought it was wonderful that the inclusion of women in social production was seen as a major milestone on the way to the liberation of women. It was an important start for the development of the women's movement and by participating in social production great self-confidence has developed among most women. Women will not return to the kitchen, to the restrictions of the household - not the women in Nepal either.

In this connection the mistakes of the old German social democratic movement were also discussed. Ferdinand Lasalle (1863) spoke against women working in factories, he gave them a place in the household. This led to fierce discussions in the social democratic movement. If Lassalle's position had been accepted, the workers' movement in the second half of the 19th century would have spoken against the liberation of women.

ANWA and the NCP (Mashal) draw lessons from this for their own discussions among the left-wing forces in Nepal. For example:

"In Nepal not only the reactionary and conservative people, but also many left-organizations and their followers also have various types of negative thinking regarding the just demands of women. Nepal Workers and Peasants Party is worth a mention in this regard. This group has constantly objected to the demand for equal property right for women. It is because of their objection that the demand for equal property right to women could not be included in the demands of 9 or 10 left groups.... This can be compared with the rejection of voting rights to women in German socialist-democratic party's conference in last century. The workers of the Nepal Communist party (Mashal) too are influenced by conservative outlook to some extent. NCP(Mashal) does not hide, but publicly criticizes such way of thinking of the party workers and gives emphasis to improve this."

Lessons are clearly drawn from the experiences of the international workers' and women's movement. Economic independence is a major step in the fight for the liberation of women. We must consistently take every step on this path. For this it is necessary to think about the effect of traditional ideas in our own minds and to conduct a consistent discussion in solidarity on this. The whole journey with the representatives of NPF and ANWA has shown that these are not just words but that criticism and self-criticism are made in an open way for the work to advance.

In the paper the success of the UNO resolutions on women's equality were also closely examined. The evaluation showed that although the UN has passed very important, far-reaching resolutions for women, the actual situation of women is still very far away from these resolutions, particularly in the developing countries.

The effects of the international women's movement on the situation of women in Nepal is vividly described. The international women's movement can really be experienced:

"The condition of Women in Nepal too is not as it was before. There has been many changes or improvement in their condition. But many of such changes have been result of international influence too. This step of Junga Bahadur was the outcome of international happenings and movements.[9] There are many examples of this type. The reforms made in the position of women in Nepal are also influenced by international progressive thoughts and revolutionary movements. Apart from Marxism-Leninism, socialism and their doctrines and international communist

9. *Jung Bahadur Rana was the founder of absolute Rana dynasty, which was abolished in 1951. He had abolished the Sati Pratha, a practice of an immolation of women in Hindu society after the death of her husband.*

movement, the proclamation about women made by the UNO also has equally influenced this women liberation movement. These examples further clarify that there is a very close connection between the women movement in Nepal and International women's movement.

To conclude, we'd like to clarify that this Charter represents only a phase of Nepal's and the world's women liberation movement. But this itself will not provide complete freedom and equality to women. Their real and complete liberation will be possible only on the basis of united movement of all exploited, oppressed people of the world including Nepal and the end of the existing society based upon exploitation and suppression as a whole. All of the exploited and oppressed people are marching towards that goal and women's liberation movement also is a part of that. We are convinced that in the last women together with all exploited and suppressed people of Nepal and whole world will be able to achieve that goal."

I fully share this optimism of our new friends. A fighting, international women's movement, which develops a clear theoretical foundation, exchanges ideas and experiences, learns from each other, has a network and unites with the international liberation movements and the workers' movement, will win the fight for the liberation of women.[10]

We Have Met the Future Women's Movement of Nepal

No matter where we went, children, especially girls, immediately appeared. They approached us inquisitively, wanted to know where we came from and why we were there. Their interest in getting to know us and our country was almost insatiable. Self-confidently they spoke to us in English which they almost all learn at school at an early age. And often we had to ask them to slow down and speak more slowly because we did not speak English as fluently as them. They were happy to help and spoke more slowly.

During the journey I realised that these self-confident girls, eager for knowledge, are the future of the fighting, Nepalese women's movement.

There were the girls from Kapilvastu on the way to the Campaign team at the very start of our journey. They, of course, got up with us at 5 a.m. so that they would not miss anything. When the Jeep would not start and we had to wait for another one, they took me by the hand, showed

---

10. *Full text of the comment made by Gabi in the remise on the paper written by com. M.B. Singh is given in Appendix-F, Page 169.*

me everything around the house and I had my first lesson in Nepali. We laughed a lot because my language skills are not the best.

There are the many letters to my daughter from girls who would love to have a pen-friend and asked Sara so many questions about Germany, the situation of girls in Germany but who are also proud to talk about their own country that has wonderful mountains, a beautiful environment but does not give them the possibility to live well.

There was Nirmala's daughter who told me, when we said goodbye, that she had played truant one day in order to be together with us. Just like her mother, she had followed us on her bicycle to the meetings for as long as she could. Only with a lot of effort could her mother prevent her from sleeping with us in her parents' bed when we were guests at her parents' home. When we said farewell, she insisted on giving me two sweets which for her were something really precious.

An then there were the many children of the successful team from Dharapani.

We got to this village the evening before the planned meeting. I had decided to present the women with a few of our songs after they had always sung to us in the Jeep as we drove along. I had managed to persuade Thomas and he assured me he would not suddenly refuse to sing. But that would have been better! They patiently listened to us singing but their polite, expressionless faces showed us that they had not enjoyed it. From then on Thomas was only allowed to hum and that was a good decision. But we had managed to achieve something. 20 children were suddenly gathered around us and they wanted to hear more and more songs and also they sang some songs in English. We spent a wonderful evening singing together in the light of the torches. Finally I sang the song "Little hands, little fists" and the children quickly learnt to sing the chorus.

I translated the verses of this song for them which tells how Carlos has to clean the shoes of rich people in Bogota, how Martha begs in the streets of Santiago and how the situation of children and girls is very similar all over the world. But also how children here learn for their lives and learn to stand up for themselves. It became clear to me that all these children could add a similar verse from their own lives. It was so moving how the children enthusiastically sang the refrain louder and louder.

**"The children of the world fighting to survive.
But in their little hands is power for a better life."**

"DON'T PLAY WITH OUR FUTURE".

Don't play with our future

Kapilvastu: the annual school exam nation

Mass meeting on the Campaign at the top of Okharkot (Pyuthan) with 650 people.

People getting down after the meeting at the top of Okharkot (Pyuthan)

The Greetings from the Women of Germany

Dear women and girls of Nepal,

My name is Sara. I want to tell you something about my life. I live in a medium size town (127,000 inhabitants) in the west of Germany. The town is called Recklinghausen. I am the daughter of Gabi who is visiting you at the moment. I am now 16 years old and still go to school. I am in the 10th class. This class is very important because after the 10th class a decision will be taken on whether I go to work or continue at school. Pupils can only continue going to school if they are good enough. At the moment I have to work very hard at school because I want to stay on at school. I just cannot imagine that children cannot go to school. In Germany school is compulsory (10 years). Sometimes it is no fun going to school. Lessons are just theoretical and then very boring: They have little to do with real life. There are so many professions and many of us just have no idea what we want to do. In Germany it is difficult for girls to find a profession in which you earn enough money to live an independent life. Lots of girls from my class want to become hairdressers. That is the lowest paid job. The pay does not allow you to live independently.

At my school there are a lot of children from many different countries; there are at least 15 different nationalities. There are no real problems because of the different nationalities and we get on well. Lots of my friends also have a job to earn some pocket money.

In my free time I always meet friends. We don't do anything special. We either walk or drive around. One friend has to take his father's company car to buy things and we help him. We have nothing else to do except wander around the streets because there are hardly any youth centers.

In January I was with two friends and the Rebells in Berlin at the Lenin, Liebknecht and Luxemburg demonstration. This was a demonstration in honour of these revolutionaries and for genuine socialism. The unity at the demonstration was good and it was marvellous to see that so many people are interested in socialism.

What is it like in Nepal ? What do young people in Nepal do in their free time (if they have any)? Are you interested in pen friends?

Sara

Dear women of Nepal

I send my kind regards to you and in this letter I want to tell you something about my life.

I am fifty years old and my name is Monika. There are more than four mil-lions unemployed people in Germany. I will to belong to them soon, because my one-year employment contract ends on March 14th. I was married until five years ago and took care of my family with two children. Now I live alone with my 14 year old daughter and urgently need work. Unfortunately I have not got any vocational training: But nowadays in Ger-many it is necessary to have some to get a job. It is the same problem with the age. Women and men over 40 have hardly a chance to find work. Actually, there is enough work in various companies and institutions, but the bosses refuse to create jobs. That is why many people become mentally and even physically ill. The employers do not care about this fact. These many sick people become desperate because they do not get suitable help. There is no money for that, we hear from the health insurance, companies and doctors. It is every humans right to have a dignified existence. We struggle for that every day. For five years I have been in a women's federation named, "Cour-age". It is financially independent, democratic, politically independent and in-ternational.

Many women meet there, to discuss problems and help each other. Through "Courage" I learned to struggle sometimes. I do not only think of me, but of my children. I also stand up for the rights of all people, so that we will not be thrown back by the aggravations of laws.

Our common protest against the often inhuman government has already con-vinced many women. We all need much courage so that we do not watch helplessly.

I wish you all good luck, hope and courage for the struggle, for that we can live together in a better world.

Yours sincerely Monika

(118)

Hallo,

My name is Rosetta. I'm twenty-five years old and I live in Herne.

My father is Italian and my mother is German. I study social work at the University of Dortmund. I like the subject because it is very interesting and varied. The course normally last nine semesters but I am in the thirteenth semester and now it is necessary to finish my studies. At the moment I am writing my dissertation.

Sometimes I worry about not finding a job after I finish because many people are unemployed especially in the social field. I live with my parents. I am quite happy to be single but lots of people can't understand this. They think it's strange if a twenty-five year old woman does not have a boyfriend But I feel good and that's the most important thing.

I have a job at gym. I work behind the bar and it's a lot of fun. I spend the money I earn ongoing to the discotheque, books, music, seminars that interest me. I pay for my clothes and my studies.

I also dance in a jazz dance group with other girls.

Another hobby is my women's group, Courage. We are women of different nationalities, ages and profession. It's interesting to be together with so many different women and we learn from each other and help each other. A very important aspect is that we are not part of a political party. Unfortunately I know a lot of people, even women, who cannot understand that I am in a women's, group. They think that women organised in a group hate men, are frustrated or are all lesbians. But these are just prejudices and sometimes I get sick of defending myself just because I am in a women's group. Fortunately not everybody thinks the same way.

For the future I hope to be able to live an independent life. That is very important for me.

Best wishes from Germany

Yours, Rosetta

Dear women of Nepal,

My name is Margin, I am 41 years old and for the last 6 years single mother of two children. My daughter Agnes is 17 years old, and Paul, my son, is 2o years old.

I'm very glad, that I'm able to send you a letter about my life in Germany. 15 years ago we left our home country Poland and came to

(119)

Germany in the hope of building a better position and a future without problems for our family. But the dreams we had came to nothing in a short time. New problems confronted us; with the language, with work and with money. To forget the problems, my husband started drinking alcohol. That's why our marriage is dissolved. After our divorce my health got very bad my husband left enormous debts for me. Only the thought that I'm not alone but have two children gave me energy and courage to live. I was brought up in a Catholic family: the woman always has to obey the husband. But throughout all the years in Germany I changed very much and I learned that women have to possess the same rights as men.

Today I work in a factory. We do shift work around the clock (changing weekly 6 a.m. until 2 p. m. / 2 p. m. until /10 in the evening / 10 in the evening until 6 a.m.).

We produce components for the car industry. In this factory 1200 people are employed, mostly women. To do shift work and piecework is bad for the health, you get disturbed sleep, stomach troubles and so on.

I earn about 1450 Euro per month (about 2800 DM). Perhaps that sounds very much, but the money is only enough for necessities. For example, the rent for the flat takes half of my wage. Especially now, after the changing from DM into Euro currency, the costs of living has gone up. Some years ago I got to know my present partner in life. He supports me very much and gave me new courage to live and energy for my further life. I hope, you liked this report from a single mother from Germany. My family and me wish you and us, that we hear and learn more from each other.

Many greetings Margit

I send warm greetings to women in Nepal

My name is Cornelia. My sister-in-law Gabi has asked me to tell you something about my lie. I am 37 years old, have been married for 16 years and have two sons who are 2 and 16 years old. My father worked for a mining company and my mother was a housewife. I have an older sister called Marion. We had a happy childhood even though my parents were not rich. I was not very successful at school but I did manage to leave school with a proper school leaving certificate. It was riot until later that I realized how fortunate one is if one has the opportunity to have a good education. That is why I attended school in the evening to get the highest German school leaving certificate. When I was 17 I started an apprenticeship as an electrician but I did not complete it because the firm which was training me went bankrupt. As a girl I did not find another firm that would train me for a job that is normally done by men and so I did all sorts of jobs to earn a living when I was 18 I met my husband. When I was 20 we got married and when I was 21 our son Bastion was born. I spent the next three years raising him. In 1986, the year our son was born, child rearing allowance was introduced in Germany. In the first two years after the birth of a child parents receive financial support. The amount depends on the parents' income. Either the father or the mother can claim the allowance, depending on who has the higher income. When Bastion started kindergarten, I was able to go to work in the mornings and I went to school in the evenings. This was a difficult tune for my husband because he was at work all day and in the evening he had to look after our son. But for me it was also very difficult. After evening school I worked in various jobs for example as a chamber maid in a small hotel. In 1997 I started training as a geriatric nurse. This is a nice profession but the conditions leave much to be desired. The old people's homes do not have enough staff so that even though the old people are clean and have enough to eat, they do not have enough activities and do not get enough attention. This is a sad side four civilised world. Before I took my examination, my son Joshua was born in February 2000. Without the support of my family it would have been very difficult to cope with my baby and do the exams. At the moment I still receive child rearing allowance but in March I will have to go back to work. I'm going back to work again because it will help us financially but also to get out of the house a bit. For me it is not enough just to do housework and raise children. I like living in Germany. We are not rich but we are happy. We have everything we need. We have a nice house, enough to eat, enough to wear and a little bit of luxury; no, actually quite a lot of luxury. What concerns me is that this does not apply to everyone here. There are lots of people who are not satisfied with their lives. People do not often speak about the this side of life in Germany. Nobody has to go hungry; if you are ill you receive medical attention. Even if you have no work, you can still live. These are things that people do not appreciate in an affluent society. That is how it often appears. I hope that when Gabi comes back she will be able to tell us a lot of things about Nepal that we do not hear or read about in the media.

My very best wishes,

Cornelia

Dear women of Nepal,

My name is Wilma. I am a farmer. Our land covers about 30 hectares and we have 24 cows.

Unfortunately my husband is ill and so we had to sell some cows. Our two daughters are married and do not live with us. We start work in the stable at 6.30 a.m. and we finish at 7.30 p.m. We also have to work at the weekends and never take a holiday. When my husband turned 60 we took a three-day trip. We think we will work for another five years and then give up our farm. My greatest fear is that I may become ill. Then we would need someone to assist us but the health insurance keeps reducing financial support for assistance.

There are lots of regulations in agriculture. The problem is that you are forced to keep a very large number of cows or else you have to give up your farm. You cannot exist with just a small farm. In order to be competitive you have to renew your machines but machines are very expensive. Only the very big farms get aid from the government. That means that you have to borrow money from the bank and then you are dependent on the bank. Normal farmers cannot work this way. There are many tragic situations because it is very hard to exist. Many families have had to give up their farms.

Our minister of agriculture, Ms Künast, made us great promises but the agricultural reforms give preference to the large-scale farming industry which has a lot of money. This frightens me. A farmer in another village now grows organic vegetables. He has to work very hard and his income is very low. Civil servants lay down laws that affect your life and you have no influence. Recently I complained about a new order but the officer just laughed at me. My husband said that I should be careful as we are dependent on this officer. But three days later I complained again. I got exact information on the order given by a professor of agriculture and he admitted defeat. Some days ago in the church choir, our priest collected signatures for a petition against the discharge of 400 workers at a factory. I supported the petition because if the workers have to save on food, it will also affect us farmers.

My best wishes,

Wilma

Hello,

My name is Ulja. I am 26 years old and live together with my partner in Gelsenkirchen which is a town located in the Ruhr, the biggest industrial area in Germany.

I work as a industrial-electioneer for a company which, among other things, produces radiators and air conditioning systems for building complexes, swimming pools, etc. I like my work very much. I have to test circuit boards controls, look for and remove the causes of defects if they are faulty.

I trained at the car manufacturer Daimler-Benz (today Daimler-Chrysler). The training was at a very high technical level. I had to study very hard primarily because we had to work independently and find solutions to problems. The colleagues in my department are all men. But the circuit boards are produced exclusively by women. The components are very small and you have to be dexterous and very fast. My colleagues get very little pay for this work. Until recently I was also paid less than my male colleagues although we all do the same work. Now at last I am paid wages at a level in accordance with my technical training and get at least as much as the colleagues in the lowest wage group. I was able to achieve this because my colleagues supported me. Although I like children very much I would not like to have any children of my own. I help children and young people a lot and support the youth organisation Rebell in its work. If I had children of my own, I would have to limit this work a lot and pass on the responsibility that I have taken on to others. I feel responsible for the future of the children of the workers and citizens and would like to invest my energy in helping them.

It is hardly possible to feed a whole family on one salary. For this reason many of my colleagues do not have any children or at the most just one child.

Best wishes

Ulja

Dear women of Nepal,

Gabi asked me to write some words about my life as a woman in Germany. It's not easy for me to write something because I don't know anything about women in Nepal and my English is bad but I want to try.

My name is Marita and I am 38 years old. I have been married since 1981 and I have 2 children who are 18 and 20 years old

When I got married in 1981 I was 17 years old In Germany it is unusual to get married at such a young age. At that time my friends still went to school or were starting to go to work but I was already a mother and I had to look after my children. My husband was very young too. We were poor people in a rich country because we had no money, no job and no qualifications. My husband was often unemployed. There were no jobs if you had no qualifications. But we were hopeful. We wanted to change our situation. My husband started working in hard jobs, often 12-13 hours a day and in the evening he went to school. It was a hard time for us. When both children went to playschool, my husband started training and I had a job for 2 hours a day, a cleaning job in a hospital. In the year 1990 our life changed. My husband got a job at Opel which belongs to General Motors and we had much more money. So I went to school for three and a half years, too. Then I studied social work. Now 11 years later I work 5 hours a day, my children are grown up and my husband has a good job, too. It took us 20 years and a lot of hard work but now we are happy. In summer we want to take our first holiday by plane. I hope you will understand me and Gabi will tell us about her journey to Nepal.

Best wishes

Marita

Dear women of Nepal,

My name is Slavica. I was born in 1951 in Sovske Dol, a village in the former Yugoslavia. I lived together with my parents on a farm and grew up with five brothers and sisters. They were all older than me. I went to school for eight years and during this time I also had to help my parents and work on the farm. I had to do the cooking or look after the cows and pigs or work in the fields.

When I was 17 I decided to take my life into my own hands and look for a different way of life. I thought I should go to another country to fulfil my objectives. The country of my choice was Germany because many people from my village had gone there. And on 22 January 1969 I actually moved without any knowledge of the language and without any money I first went to a town called Gutersloh.

There I worked in a clothes factory for a year. After this I changed my job and worked in the kitchen of a clinic. I met my husband and married him on 15 September 1973. After we got married we moved to Recklinghausen. After a long search I managed to find a suitable job there. I again worked in a kitchen, this time in an old people's home. In 1977 my daughter was born. That year I also changed my job and started working for a supplier of car parts. I have been working at the same place for 24 years. In 1983 our second daughter was born.

Best wishes,

Slavica

Dear Women of Nepal,

My name is Agnes. I would like to tell you that also in Germany exploitation of women is quite common.

I work at a company where I am totally underpaid. My pay is clearly lower than my male colleagues who work with me.

Even if f they go to the hairdresser's women have to pay much more than men for the same service. There are also men who have their hair permed or dyed. I am divorced and have 3 grown-up children. My ex-husband and I owned a house together. When our property was divided up it was agreed that I would give up the house and get DM 15,00o compensation. I agreed to this because any more disputes over money would have meant that the lawyers would have charged even more. I now know that I made a mistake. At that time two banks that financed the house were not mentioned at the divorce. Since the divorce my former husband has become unemployed and has stopped paying for the house. There are still outstanding debts of DM 75,000 on the house. As we are divorced I think that the debts have nothing to do with me. But the banks have a different view. They think that I should repay the loans or else they threaten to take me to court. There is a second loan which they also want me to repay. They want DM 590 a month. I agreed to DM 200 a month and have written to the bank that my exhusband lives in the house and that it belongs to him alone. I told them that they should write to him. I am taking my husband to court because of the loans on the house. My lawyer told me that I would lose any case against the banks and that I have a 50:50 chance against my husband.

(125)

While I was married I did not work for 10 years. This means that when I retire I will get a small share of my husband's pension. My own pension will not be high because of the ten years that I did not pay into the pension insurance. That is my situation. There are many other women who are in similar situations to me.

My warmest greetings

Agnes

Dear friends,

Sincere greetings from Germany to you women and girls from Nepal

My name is Heike and I live in a small town with about 70,000 inhabitants. I am 46 years old, married and have two children. My daughter is 23 and my son 16. I love them both very much. Don't laugh, but I am in my third marriage. Unfortunately I was not lucky with my first two husbands. My third marriage is very happy and my children like their stepfather very much. When I got divorced my children were very young I brought them up alone.

I'm a geriatric nurse. I don't know, if this job exists in your country. I think in Nepal the people live in extended families. There the elderly and sick people are no doubt looked after by their families, which is not always easy I think. In your country we have old-age homes, were old people live and are looked after by nurses. Rooms in this homes are very expensive, and there are not enough nurses. The owners of the homes do not want to employ more nurses.

Therefore we do not have enough time to look after the elderly. It has always made me angry to have no time for these people. I have a lot of arguments with my boss. We cannot just wash the people and feed them. They need also love, respect, talks and a lot of fresh air: These old people gave us life, looked after us, lived through two wars, rebuilt Germany. There was some bad things, but a lot of good things. We have to be grateful to them. But we have a system, where only money and profit are important. You can earn nothing from old people.

Two years ago I stopped working, I have an illness, which doesn't allow me to work any more. I miss my job. It will not be easy for me to train for a new job and to work. With the high unemployment I am almost too old.

At the moment I do the housework. In the past we shared it.

We have a garden which I love. We have a lot of flowers, a pond, bushes fruit trees and vegetables. Unfortunately it is winder. I am looking forward to spring When I have time, I am often in the garden. My husband and I like nature. !n the garden we have a lot of birds, insects and fish. We watch them, enjoy it and get a lot of positive strength. My husband Christoph and I are partners, not only in the garden. We both do political work. We believe and work for a system without exploitation and oppression. I would like everyone in the world have the same chances. Technology can make it possible. Nobody in the word needs to suffer hunger.

Dear friends, I could write so much. I am sure that Gabi will tell a lot about you. I am happy about the exchange with you and my friends.

I embrace you all, I with you and your families health and strength.

Heike.

Hello, dear nepalese women,

A very lovely hello from Herne in Germany! I am glad to be able to write you this letter and I look forward to what Gabi will tell me about your life.

My name is Klaudia, I am 47 years old, divorced and have two sons. There ages are 22 and 21. They both study. I grew up with two brother and sisters, in poor family relations. My father was a bricklayer and after the second word war he fled from East Prussia. He worked very hand and died at 55. He had cancer. When I was 15, I met my ex-husband. I married when I was 21. My School education was very good I had 10 years of school, and went to what the call the middle school here. I had a commercial apprenticeship in a coal-mine. After that, I worked in the telephone exchange shift work. I started work their 27 years ago, enjoyed the work from the beginning, and have stayed there until now. Now have been in this men dominated area for 30 years, in the mines, which are supposedly being doing so bad. Today we are only 50.00o employees and in the next year they plan to reduce to 35,000. So the pressure and our work is 8 hours hander than ever. In the age of 27 and 28 our 2 little, sweet sons were born. My former husband was a strong drinker, and smoker. Therefore I needed a childminder for my sons. There are no day-care nurseries for shift workers here.

We bought an little house when the children were 1 and 2 years old. We had a lot to pay for the down-payments for this house, even though we paid less taxes in the first years. And in addition to this, the childminder.

When my sons were 6 and 7, my husband left us, he was not happy with us, was his opinion. That took me down. Now I had a lot of debts and two hyperactive sons. I had to make out without a childminder. My money often was not enough to buy us enough to eat and drink. It was very hard for me. When I came home from work at lo p.m., the house looked like someone had thrown a bomb in it. I often cleaned up half the night, and was on my feet for 16 hours. Sometimes the father took his sons for the weekend Depending on his mood. My father died the same year that my ex husband moved out. My mother moved to the coast, to another man. I didn't have many friends or help by neighbors. Here in Germany, many people an so busy with themselves that nobody can help anybody else. My sister looked after the boys, especially when I was on late shift and gave me 10 or 20 Euros once in a while. At the same time, she was scolding. 8 years ago I met the Courage women and also Gaby through a newspaper article. Thus I learned that one can live and think differently than the "idealism" that is so highly thought of here. At the telephone exchange at work there is naturally a lot of stress. A different shift every day, I had to be ready to go back to work on my free days and on holidays. 2 porters have been layed off and I have to do their work as well. It is often almost too much to take. Every time one is ill, there are huge mobbing attacks. They want to get rid of us. We are supposedly too expensive. From 150.000 employees reduced to 35.000, and at the same time with the same amount of work to be done. Often I am not able to do all my work. My boys are studying engineering: Due to a new law, I have to pay more taxes now, as much as a single has to pay. On the weekends, I work in a big disco cleaning toilets. Sometimes it is disgusting, but I like it nonetheless. Otherwise I would be alone at home. This way I can afford some extra things like going swimming or to the movies etc. That would not be possible only with my wages at the coal mine. And I would like to buy a car soon. It is too cold to ride a motor scooter when it gets to be-10^0 C. I want to be flexible to do work for Courage. Even though I live in the so-called "rich " prosperity, I feel "poor". Only with my Courage women do I experience closeness and friendship, respect and acceptance. The struggle against oppression is a part of this friendship and respect. it is normal for me to come to the Courage activities (which we often have to win new members) even after one or two nights of work at the disco and often 5o hours of work. I wish you in Nepal solidarity, much power and strength for our common struggle for more justice.

I send you my best wishes,

Klaudia

Appendix-B

Reply from the ANWA to the Women of Germany

Dear Friends.

All Nepal Women's Association (ANWA) is much pleased to receive letters with "Best Wishes" from the women of Germany. We are really grateful and obliged to you for all these letters.

Perhaps, it is already known to you that ANWA is going to hold an All Nepal Women National Campaign (ANWNC) for two years of which the concluding part of the first year is taking place now. At present there is emergency rule in Nepal and all fundamental rights granted by the con-stitution have been suspended. Because of it and together with the Maoist activities, terror and horror prevails every where in the country. Such a situation has compelled almost all po-litical parties, organizations or class and mass organization to holdover all their major public programs. But ANWA is de-termined to make it a success inspite of the difficulties it has to face because of the emergency rule and Maoist activities.

While we are conducting our Campaign in such a dif-ficult and critical condition, your letters, full of true fraternal feelings and hearty good wishes, give us not only much plea-sure, but also boost our moral to go ahead boldly in the Campaign. Besides it, we are much proud to have Gabi among us throughout the whole Campaign. She is marching with us in even most difficult condition. She is warmly welcomed by all people and women of Nepal everywhere she goes.

From your letters and from the message of com Gabi too, we are immensely happy to know that the law in Ger-many has given equal rights to women. That is a great achieve-ment. We Nepalese women too are struggling hard to achieve such a right for women. The achievement of German women will inspire us in our struggle for achieving equal rights to women in our Country too.

From what you have written in your letters, it is not difficult for us, to understand that you still have to go further in your liberation movement. Although women are equal to men in Germany by law, they are not still equal to men in real sense. As Gabi has mentioned in her message only a socialist revolution can completely solve the problems of freedom, equality and liberation of women. In Nepal, we are still in the stage of new democratic revolution. The Women's Liberation Movement also is a part of that revolution, i.e. new demo-critic revolution. But we are also aware that such a revolution is and should be a part of worldwide socialist revolution. Socialist revolution is a common program of the working people, exploited and suppressed women of the whole world. This common goal of socialism binds us together.

In such a background the importance of the solidarity of working class people, exploited and suppressed men of the whole world is self evident. We take the letters of Ger-man Women, the message of Gabi for Campaign, and the par-ticipation of herself together with her husband Thomas, as living symbols of international solidarity. For that we would like to extend our greeting to all revolutionary women of German on behalf of the revolutionary women of Nepal and ANWA too. We are happy to mention that ANWA is determined to further strengthen its relationship with the revolutionary women of Germany and to consolidate international solidarity with the working class people and exploited women of the whole world. We re fully confident that you will continue encouraging us in coming days too with your inspiring and enlightening suggestions and advices through letters.

With Warmest Revolutionary Greetings

Durga Paudel
President,
ANWA

Appendix-C

Charter of Women's Rights

(After one year long "Charter of Women's Rights" national Campaign, " The Charter of Women's Rights" was adopted in February1995 by second extended meeting of Central Committee of All Nepal Women's Association held in Kapilvastu in February 1995.)

Preamble

1. Men and Women, in principle are equal by birth. But they have been discriminated and victimized for long on different issues. They are almost in a stage of slavery. It is, therefore, our historical responsibility to liberate them from such a grave situation with a view to giving them their long due self-respect and rights.

2. Women's salvation is not an isolated issue, as it has its roots in the exploitative socio-political system. They can be liberated only when an exploitation –free society is created by eradicating the discriminatory system which deprives the working people the fruit of their labour and sacrifice.

3. Women's condition as it is today is the direct result of the prevailing socio-economic system. which has been in practice for a long and it serves the interest of exploiting class. So, until and unless existing unjust socio-economic structure is not subverted, women can't realize basic change in their life.

4. There are people in society who still object to giving equal rights to women in property. Similarly, some people oppose the women enjoying the rights of divorce, remarriage and widow marriage. But all these voices of opposition will disappear once the women raise the flag of revolt with full determination against all such practices. In future, women will have equal rights not only in property, but also for abortion and other such things only after long and consistent struggle. Like in the past, reactionary forces are to be defeated with tooth and nail to achieve the goals of woman's liberation.

5. Equal rights for women are appropriate only in the general senses, as they need more rights to lift them up from their miserable plight. They need special rights due to their speciality of physical state and also because of their weaknesses developed in the context of their physical and psychological condition. Moreover, today almost all social institutions, law, culture, religion and other traditions are against them due to the patriarchal social set-up. So they need different and special rights than the rights enjoyed by the men.

6. Many steps have been taken in national and international level regarding the question of Women's upliftment from their humiliating condition. International institution, including UNO, have raised voice and passed resolution in favour of Women's liberation from their slave like situation. Our own government has been no exception to all these works done in favour of women. But the women are so much dominated and exploited by the men that a lot has to be done still to free them really. Still there is much gap between the passed resolutions and the application of them in reality.

7. Overhauling the present family system is one of the pre-requisites for the liberation of Women. It is this family structure which confines the women to household works and prevents them from expressing their feelings against the discrimination in the name of gender.

8. Today there are two standards for men and women in the matter of sexual morality. Men enjoy more rights in terms of sexual questions and women have to pass through various restrictions which reveal not only the discrimination suffered by the women but also the narrow mind set up of the present social structure.

9. It is a historical fact that many changes occur in society on their own, not following the desires and orders of people. Such changes sometimes play determining role. In the Past, some changes took place in our society due to the pressure of time on the one hand, and on the other due to some some reforms initiated by the reactionary rulers, including in the Rana regime and Panchayat system. But today the situation has worsened so much that women can't be freed without initiating a determining movement against the present setup which is strongly ingrained in favour of exploiting class. Thus the Charter of Women's Rights is a step in order to arouse the public consciousness about the women's plight.

Part-I

Equal Rights in Property.

Freedom and equality to women is not possible without the economic freedom and equality. Equal rights in property for women is one of the fundamental pre-requisites to liberate women. They work more than the male, so they should be entitled to have equal rights in their earning and the parental property.

Some skeptics point out that if women are given their parents' or husbands' property, then they will go in changing their loyalty and opt for remarriage. But all these doubts are the consequences of male-dominated social set-up which doesn't accept women as equals. If women can have rights on patriarchal and husband's property, similarly men also can have rights on parential property brought by the women. If people are honest and sincere then the present laws can be changed to the satisfaction of both men and women. So, there is no room for any objection by the male in regard to giving property right to the women. If we can have cynical views on women's equal rights, same question can be applied in the case of men, because they have time and again misused their rights on parental property by marrying two or three wives. The main question is that in the case of property there should be equal rights for men and women. The following points need serious consideration in this regard :

i. Equal rights on parental property for sons and daughters

ii. After marriage, men and women must have equal rights regarding the ownership, management, consumption purchase and sale of family property.

iii. The equal right of women on the property should not be terminated even in the case of divorce, remarriage and illicit sexual relationship.

iv. The right of Women on the property must be governed by the same rules as those applied to man.

Part-II

Marriage and Right for Divorce.

The present marriage system is based in favour of men and so this is responsible for many ills and miseries in the life of women. In the name of marriage women have been facing all sorts of insults and humiliation for centuries. Women don't have outlets to escape from the trauma of divorce and other problems related to marriage. When married life becomes like a hell, then there should be provision for getting rid of such condition. In this regard the following points should be taken into consideration:

1. Marriage should be based on mutual love and feelings for each other and nothing should be done against the wishes of one party.

2. Marriage based on caste and religion must be banned and eliminated.

3. Conjugal life should be based on mutual love, respect equality and freedom

4. In case of discriminatory behaviour and injustice inflicted on her by her husband and his parents, she should be entitled to divorce or remarriage.

5. Divorce process should be very easy and inexpensive.

6. Husband or their parents should bear all the expenses during the process of divorce.

7. Women should have rights over the ownership of property even after the divorce or remarriage.

8. After divorce, there should be a provision for children's livelihood and education based on justice without any discrimination against women keeping in view of the supreme interest of the children's future.

Part-III

Right of Abortion
Pregnancy and child births are questions mainly and purely related to women. It is her private affair whether to have child or not at a particular time. She possesses a strong desire to become mother of child, but if she is in compulsion for any reason for abortion, she should have full right to opt for such abortion without any fear. These days there are various means of preventing pregnancy and also the means for abortion. These things must be available to women whenever she desires so. The argument that such a right will increase immoral people in the society is groundless. The following points should be kept in mind in this regard:

1. Women should have full rights for abortion.

2. All laws against abortion should be abolished.

3. Abortion should be easy and inexpensive affair.

4. If the women want to keep their identity secret in the case of abortion, their right should be guaranteed. There should be strong legal punishment for those who disclose their secrecy or identity.

Part-IV

Women's Sale and Prostitution

Women's sale and prostitution is on increase in our country. Unlike in the past, women are sold in other third world countries besides India. In Nepal itself prostitution is increasing. The women are sold and trapped into prostitution. It is very difficult to give them back their self-respect once they are sold or rapped.

Though the government has its own laws meant for preventing the prostitution, they are sold and used in prostitution due to the nexus between criminals and politicians. Moreover, the government cannot be strict enough in this regard as the government's tourism policy is based on luring foreign tourists who are supplied women at hotels in an secret way. So, Women's this problem can be solved only by destroying the present profit oriented capitalistic system. The following points should be taken into consideration in this regard:

1. Laws should be strict about the prostitution and sale of women.

2. Corrupt policemen and administrative officials must be punished severely.

3. Government should take measures to take back the women forced to live in foreign brothers in India and other countries.

4. Nepalese women forced to live a life of prostitute in our country or abroad must be rehabilitated suitably and appropriately.

5. Such women should be provided with all the facilities needed for their career development. The should be given training for various activities including cottage industries. They should also be given economic, assistance to start small-scale industries.

Part-V

Violence and Misbehavior against Women:

Today women in Nepal have become victim of violence and misbehavior. It starts from the home itself where they are tortured and discriminated by their own husbands and father-in-laws. In the dowry case, many women are driven out of the house. On the otherhand, women don't get justice once they are taken to courts in such cases. Police and civil administration are usually prejudiced to the cases related to women. Moreover, many women suffering from violent behaviour don't go to the course as they know that this is very expensive process beyond their capacity. The following points should be taken into consideration in this regard :

1. Stringent laws should be enacted to prevent violent behaviour, insulting treatment and rape against women.

2. There should be provision of security for women against all sorts of injustices and torture suffered at the hands of their husbands and inlaws.

3. There should be strong laws to prevent any attempt of women's character assassination.

4. There should be provision of compensation for women if they are raped or molested by the criminals.

Part-VI

Restrictions over Women's Rights :

Women are deprived of many rights. They are not only denied the rights to sell the property of their husbands and fathers, but also are prevented from visiting foreign countries without approval of their guardians. Our old tradition and custom are against them. They are victimised in various ways. So the following ways can be taken to help them.

1. Women should be given full freedom to utilise their all rights.

2. All laws preventing the women from using their rights should be scrapped.

3. It is to be guaranteed that old customs and traditions do not pose obstacles in the realization of women's rights. Social customs biased against women should be discarded.

Part-VII

Protection of the rights of the minority, oppressed and indigenous women:

Though the minority, oppressed and indigenous women are more free than the women belonging to other section of society, they are deprived of their rights its many cases. The following points should be taken very seriously.

1. Women belonging to indigenous minority sections should have the rights to enjoy their traditional rights.

2. If the traditional practices act as obstacles in the realization of women's rights, there should be provision to protect women from these traditions so that they could exercise their power.

3. There should be legal provision to protect women of minority section from the people belonging to aristocratic class.

Part-VIII

Family Court:

Until and unless the present exploitative social set up remains operative, women can't expect to get redresal to their grievances. The present social setup police, courts and other administrative institutions can't protect the women from the injustice and other criminal attacks. It is for this reason that in many countries there are family courts which are entrusted with the responsibility of safeguarding women's rights.

Following points should be given serious consideration to establish family court and protect the women from all sorts of injustice and discrimination:

1. Family courts should be established to look into and settle the questions concerning marriage, divorce, crime by the husbands, family conflicts, property disputes and other such issues.

2. At the beginning such courts should be established at district level, but slowly such courts should be opened at local level too.

3. There should be easy and inexpensive process in the family courts for all sorts of reports and their verification .

4. There should be equal proportional representation of male and female in the court.

Part-IX

Miscellaneous:

1. Women should be paid equally like their male workers for similar work.

2. Strong actions should be taken against the factory owners and others who are found responsible for inflicting inhuman treatment or perpetrating crimes on women.

3. Vulgar advertisement against women should be banned strictly.

4. Women employees should be given preference for their posting according to the convenience in terms of home and other such factors.

5. All laws having discriminatory provision should be scrapped.

6. There should be provision of reservation for women in education and employment keeping in view of their vulnerable condition and also the men's prejudice against them. They should be given scholarship and career development opportunities so that they could compete with their male counterpart in society with full confidence.

Durga Paudel
President
All Nepal Women's Association
Nepal

Appendix-D

Report on the Women's Liberation Movement of Nepal[11]

The period of last five years has remained very important and glorious period in the history of ANWA. During this period ANWA organized not only a national Campaign for the Charter of Women's Rights, it also became successful to adopt a historical resolution on it. We also have many weaknesses. One of biggest weaknesses is our inability to build a strong and nation-wide organization. Assessing our strengths and weaknesses of previous years, we need to work out on concrete programs and policies for the years to come. We have great pleasure to announce you that in order to speed the historical tradition of the Charter of Women's Rights up and give it a new height and broader shape, ANWA has introduced All Nepal Women's National Campaign 2000 and 2001 for coming two years. We are hopeful that this Campaign will give a new dimension to ANWA and its movement.

Prior to make an overview of the past five years, we think it essential to analyze the condition of women's movement in the context of national and international situation. We would like to put in a clear cut words that our movement, i.e. women's liberation movement is not a pure national movement separated from both Nepal's and World's revolutionary movement. In order to strongly push it forward correctly and actively, we, therefore, need to understand it not by isolating but by linking it to the political situation and revolutionary movement of both Nepal and the World.

The movements launched all over the world for the reforms or emancipation of the women count so much for whatever reforms or changes the Nepali women have made at present to improve their socio-economic conditions. The end of sati pratha[12] first in our neighboring country

---

11. *Extracts from the Report presented by Com. Durga Paudel, president of All Nepal Women's Association (ANWA) to the Forth National Confrence of the ANWA held in Butwal, Nepal in April 7-9, 2000 and Adopted by the Conference.*

12. *Sati is a practice of an immolation of woman in Hindu society after the death of her husband.*

India is an example of such a movement. Similarly, the experience we have gained from the women's liberation movement world over has contributed a lot to guide many our principles which we have been following in relation to our women's liberation movement. Not only the women's liberation movement, the more socialist, new-democratic or a revolutionary movement becomes stronger either in the world or in Nepal, the more it assists to our liberation movement. ANWA, therefore, always supports or keeps solidarity with revolutionary movements of the exploited and oppressed people or mass-organizations and political parties which represent them. It criticizes those ideas which try to isolate women's movement from the world movement by taking it as a purely independent feminist movement.

In those countries where there existed socialist system, important works had been done to emancipate women from traditional servitude and to provide them freedom and equality equal to that of men in every sphere of life. It makes it clear that women can get their real emancipation only in a socialist system. It is not possible in a exploitation-based system . So, change in the present exploitation-based system and replacement of it by building the socialist or exploitation free social system is also a question significantly related to the women's movement. At present, the world socialist system has collapsed and its negative impact is evident in the women's movement as well. Women's movement has greatly been damaged by the deteriorating bourgeois culture, Islamic or Roman Catholic fundamentalism and Hindu conservatism. In such a situation, advancement of women's movement is possible either by supporting or by keeping solidarity with all theoretical or cultural struggles against all forms of wrong thinking.

Nepal, at present, is in a state of semi-feudal and semi-colonial condition. The immediate solution of women's problems possible only after destroying the present condition and establishing new-democratic system. However, the real solution is only possible after the establishment of exploitation free social system. But for the time being, new-democratic system is far from our reach. There are so many problems and road blocks to get to that direction. Women do have same problems and road blocks in the direction of fulfilling our broader interest. Our duty is therefore to make maximum contribution to the new democratic movement. For that we need to keep solidarity with all leftist, revolutionary and progressive forces as well as all justice-loving people.

For the last thirty years. our country was ruled by the autocratic monarchy and fascist Panchayat System. The great historic mass movement of 1991 ousted fascist Panchayat System and introduced a limited form of multi-party system. We admit it without any hesitation that compared to the fascist period, this type of limited changes have provided women with more freedom and opportunities at least for their organizational activities, though the freedom and opportunities are very limited.

The continious activities against the present multi-party system of the royalist and retrogressive forces, on the one hand, and congressite government on the other is the major and immediate political crisis of our country. While the royalists intend to reinstate the direct and autocratic rule of the King, the congressites attempt to establish its own one-party dictatorship. If the present system is collapsed by any of these two forces, it will have negative impact on women's liberation movement or their organizational activities. Therefore, our duty is to continuously and firmly raise voices against such type of danger and to support and co-operate the movement of all forces struggling against the same danger.

As stated earlier, there is a limited form of multi-party system in the country. Although the system is quantitatively progressive than the fascist Panchayat System, eventually it is a reactionary system. This system represents mainly the reactionaries and retrogressive forces. As a result, the present government is unable even to take any preliminary steps to bring changes in the present medieval social condition of women and to constitutes laws in favor of their progressive and legitimate demands. The government, for example, is one of the signatories of UN Convention on the Elimination of All Forms of Discrimination against Women (CEDAW). But the government has not been able to take any steps, in accordance with principles of CEDAW and the directives of the Supreme Court, to improve the medieval social condition of Nepali women. Instead, due to the pressure of Conservative and retrogressive forces, the government stopped some preliminary steps taken according to the directives of Supreme Court and the bill that was tabled in the Parliament . This clearly suggests that without effective mass movement or a strong women's movement, we cannot force the government to take any steps even for preliminary reforms for women. Realizing the facts and keeping them in mind, ANWA has introduced All Nepal Women National Campaign 2000-2001 programs for the next two years. We know that the drastic change in the present condition of women is not possible under any reactionary system. However, through the strong movement based on public support, we can make the government compelled for a limited or minimal reforms.

ANWA should also independently make its maximum efforts to organize forceful movement in the country. We believe that only on the basis of a joint efforts of all women's organizations and political forces which stand in favor of progressive and legitimate demands of women, we can make the government compelled to take steps in favor of the demands of women are putting. Therefore, wherever and whenever such possibilities are available, ANWA will try to bring them in their favor or it will support the movement organized even by others for the same cause. But in doing so, there are too many difficulties and problems. The nine Left political parties and organisations involved in their united movement, for instance, have not clearly presented the demand of equal property rights to women while presenting their 34 point demands to the government. They are unable to do so because the code of conduct of the united movement. According to the code of conduct, if any party disagrees with any issue for some reasons, the others cannot endorse it. As an organisation had objection to equal property rights to the women, the demand of equal property rights to women was not included in the list of the nine left parties. The question of equal property rights to women has been supported by all Marxist-Leninists throughout the world. But the disagreement among the Nepali political parties and organisations who claim themselves as communists, in relation to equal property rights to women is a matter of grave sorrow. We also do not find any essential clarity among some of the so-called left parties or women's organization closer to them about those struggles which are targeted against agencies of imperialism and/or various NGOs and INGOs directed by imperialist forces or various agencies attached to them. This has created many obstacles for a joint movement of women. Despite the fact there are possibilities for a joint-struggle on certain issues, there are also many difficulties to push a joint movement ahead in totality. Therefore, ANWA should make its every effort to speed the women's joint- movement up on several possible issues. At the same time, it should also initiate its own independent movement.

While fighting for women's rights, freedom and equality as well as against the danger for multi-party system, we should not ignore the danger that comes from foreign aggression against the nationality and sovereignty of our country. There is a growing amount of danger from the US imperialism and primarily from the Indian expansionism in particular to our nationality and sovereignty. The encroachment, intervention and hegemony of the Indian expansionism are increasing each day in our territory, economy, industry, commerce, water resources and administration. The US imperialism and the financial institutions associated with it are working in a planned way, to hold Nepal under their sway.

From the descriptions we have made earlier so far in relation to the national and international contexts, it is crystal clear that the women's movement is not that straight and easy as we see it externally. On the contrary, there are so many complexities and hardships. Therefore, in such a situation it will be possible for us to advance women's movement in a proper and forcible way only by adopting a clear-cut theoretical outlook and raising the women's consciousness to a higher level.

II. Evaluation of the Past

I. Achievements

The glorious years of women's movement

With regard to the evaluation of the past, first of all, the evaluation of the three and half years period, beginning on 29-30 November 1992 through 28 May 1996 is very important. It is very important not only in the history of ANWA, but also in the history of Nepal's women's movement as a whole. During that period, first, the extended meeting of ANWA held on 29-30 November 1992 at Butwal approved the resolution of equal property rights to women. On the same occasion, for the first time in the history of ANWA, it organized a massive street demonstration at Butwal Bazar demanding equal property rights to women.

The resolution on 'equal rights to women" adopted by the extended meeting reads as:

1. Equal rights should be given to both son and daughter in patrimonial property.

2. Equal rights should be given to both husband and wife to buy and sell or to manage their properties.

3. Those who do not have son, they should give all of their properties to their daughters.

4. Women's property rights should not be dismissed if she is alleged or found guilty of adultery or immoral character.

5. Equal property rights on a joint-properties should be given to a woman even in a condition that she legally or otherwise separates herself from her husband.

6. If a woman dissatisfies with her husband or with his family, she should be given a full rights to live single with her properties, sale her properties or take her properties with her even if she gets her second marriage

7. If a woman gets second marriage without legal divorce, her former husband or his family's claim to compensate the amount of their marriage expenses (jewelry and other expenses) from her parental family should stop completely .

8. A widow should enjoy full property rights to their joint properties. There should not be any obstacles to the property rights to the widow due to the death of her husband.

Based on these resolutions, ANWA made its continuous efforts in a planned way to push women's struggle ahead for equal property rights.

In order to raise the same issue more forcefully and push the struggle ahead, a symposium on the question of "Equal rights to Women" was organized. The symposium was divided into three phases. The first phase was organized at the village level, the second at the district level and the third one at the national level. The symposium run for three months and it was of its own kind on the same issue. The symposium was participated by thousands of women, intellectuals and people of different strata. Finally, on 20 Feb. 1995, the symposium was organized at national level in Kathmandu. On that occasion working-papers were presented on three different sub-topics:

1. Women's Liberation Movement and the question of equal property rights to women.

2. International Women's movement and question of equal property rights to women.

3. Laws and Acts in Nepal and the question of equal property rights to women.

In June, 1994, Mahila Dhoni[13] was published as special issue of "Equal Property Rights to Women". In the same year, the third national conference of ANWA was held on 22-24 March. The major slogan of the conference was, on and daughter are equal, property should be equal to them. On the basis of the slogan, a huge mass demonstration was organized at Butwal.

ANWA also decided to launch a Campaign for all sorts of rights to women raising high slogan of equal property rights to women making qualitative progress. According to this, the second extended meeting of the third committee of ANWA held on 9-10 Feb., 1995 at Kusma and Kapilbastu decided to run a year long program entitled "Women's Charter of Rights National Campaign". This Campaign lasted to the end of March, 1996. This program was divided into 4 Phases. The first phase concluded various programs. These are:

1. The formation of the central Campaign running committee,

2. Publication and distribution of the resolution of the charter of women rights national Campaign,

3. Advocating, wall painting, financial collection, and press meet in Kathmandu.

In the second phase, district level meetings of women, wide scale propagative and preparatory works and organizational activities were completed successfully. Similarly, in the third phase, collection of suggestions, meetings with journalists, intellectuals and various organizations with regards to the Charter of Women's Rights completed at the national level. In order to complete these tasks, women activists had traveled many parts of the Nepal and India.

In the fourth phase, on 25-26 Jan., 1995 a round-table conference was held in Kathmandu to conduct discussion on the topic pertaining to the Charter of Women's Rights. Four agendas were presented to discuss during the round table conference. There were: (1) the question of women's equal rights to property, (2) trafficking of women and prostitution, (3) marriage and divorce and (4) the question of abortion. Women intellectuals, journalists, lawyers, politicians and social workers in a large number participated in the round table conference. Following the round table

---

13. *Mahila is women and dhoni is sound or voice. Thus, Mahila dhoni is Women's Voice.*

conference, there was a demonstration of women in Kathmandu demanding not only equal property rights to women but also asking the government for many other demands as well. After one year's extensive preparation, the third extended meeting of Central Committee held on 23-24 Jan., 1995 Butwal adopted the resolution on the Charter of Women's Rights. The ch. rter itself is a great historical document of women's liberation movement in Nepal. Excluding the preamble, the document contains the following nine chapters:

1. Equal property rights to women.

2. Freedom of marriage and separation or divorce.

3. Freedom of abortion.

4. Control of women trafficking and prostitution.

5. Control over malpractice and criminal activities against women.

6. End of control over women's rights

7. Protection of rights of women from minority, oppressed (untouchables[14]) and other ethnic groups.

8. Family Court

9. Miscellaneous

The Charter of Women's Rights has materialized the demands of women's liberation movement which is going for a long time to achieve freedom and equality as enjoyed by the men. The document has greatly contributed to speed up, uplift and complete the historical tradition of the "Manifesto of All Nepal Women Association" adopted by the second national conference of the association held clandestinely in 1988 at Gorakhpur, India. At the same time, the document has provided a strong theoretical ground to the women's liberation movement of Nepal. After approving the document, a signature Campaign was organized to win the public support in favor of the document both at home and abroad. After getting thousands of signatures of both men and women, it was presented to the prime minister as a memorandum. The third extended meeting of the central committee of ANWA held on 24-25 Jan., 1995 decided to mark the 25th January as Women's Rights Day. The conference proposes to observe the 25th of January as the Women's Rights Day on a regular basis.

---

14. *Untouchables are tradtional occupational caste groups. They fall at the bottom of the Hindu social hierarchy.*

In order to legalize the Charter of Women's rights approved by ANWA, Com. Navraj Subedi, General Secretary of National People's Front and Member of the House of Representatives registered a non-governmental bill at the Parliament Secretariat on April 7, 1997. This bill aims to provide Nepali women with complete freedom and equality by eliminating all forms of discrimination against them. Com Subedi registered the same bill for several times in 1998 and 1999. Com Dila Ram Acharya, Member of the House of Representatives and Advisor to National Peoples' Front also registered the same bill again in 2000. But, the government has not yet presented it to the Parliament for discussion. Due to increasing amount of pressure of the women's movement for their rights, privileges, freedom and equality, the government proposed to introduce a new bill that would null and void all sort of discriminatory laws and acts against women. But the proposed bill made very limited provisions towards ending the discriminations against women. All the reactionary and retrogative forces raised their voices against it. But ANWA decided to support the bill critically and demanded its presentation to the Parliament without delay. In order to put more pressure to the government, ANWA organized a press conference and a interaction program on June and July 6 of 1996.

In short, the period of three and half years beginning in 9 Dec., 1993 through 28 May, 1996 has been the period of glorious years in the history of women's liberation movement of Nepal. By this time, we need to put our efforts to reach our movement to a new height by preparing concrete programs......

A : Immediate Demands

The organization of a broad-based women's movement is an urgent need to eliminate all forms of discrimination against women. Similar movement for the legitimate demands of women is also equally urgent We should try to organize such types of movement on the basis of the "Charter of Women's Rights" adopted in 1996. For the time being, we should put our efforts to organize our movement on the ground of following demands:

1. Women should enjoy equal property rights to that of man.

2. All forms of discriminatory Laws and Acts against women should be abolished.

(147)

3. Strong provision of punishment against rape, abusing and teasing of women should be made.

4. There should be an effective legal provision for protection and justice for women against beating, torture and abuse within the family.

5. Laws, Acts and social codes that discriminate woman against man with regard to divorce, marriage, morality and social conduct should be ended.

6. The social practices that restrict marriage on the bases of caste and religion should be avoided.

7. Legal provision should be made for strict punishment against any kinds of back-biting and teasing which destroy the personal character of woman.

8. Women should enjoy the rights of divorce with her property if she is tortured and ill-treated by the family.

9. The traditional freedom enjoyed by the women from minority, oppressed (untouchables) and ethnic groups should be protected.

10. Legal provisions should be made against those customary practices if they violate the rights of women from minority, oppressed and ethnic groups.

11. Strong legal and administrative provisions should be made if people from upper caste and classes interfere the rights of women from minority, oppressed and ethnic groups.

12. A separate family court should be established to probe and prosecute the family cases of women.

13. Women should be paid equal wages for equal works.

14. Strong legal provision of punishment should be made if working women are humiliated and malpracticed by their employers.

15. No matter whether she is permanently or temporarily employed, a working women should get al essential expenses and/or compensation if she suffer from illness, get injured or died during her employment period in any industry or firm .

16. There should be restriction upon the obscene use of women for any kinds of advertisement.

17. There should be restriction on beauty contest.

18. Strong steps should be taken in order to control women's trafficking.

19. Considering the motherhood and biological features of women, they should enjoy special privileges and protection.

20. Reservation of seats should be made for women in education, employment and other social service sectors.

21. Women should enjoy full freedom of reproduction and abortion.

22. The children above the age of 5 and under the age of 12 should be given 50% concession while traveling by bus.

23. In accordance with the directives of the Supreme Court, a bill for the abolition of all forms of discrimination against women should be introduced in the parliament and approved by it soon .

24. The government should take a serious step without delay to implement CEDAW and aftertreaties concerning the rights of women and other treaties concerning the rights of women adopted by the UN and endorsed by the Nepal government itself.

B : Immediate Policies and Activities

Immediately, ANWA determines the following policies and actions:

1. Awareness and Public Opinion: Advancing the historic legacy of the Charter of Women's Rights National Campaign, ANWA decides to run "All Nepal Women's National Campaign 2000/2001" for the coming two years with the following objectives:

(a) to raise consciousness and create nationwide public opinion among women about their legitimate demands and the Charter of Women's Rights.

(b) To put pressure to the government to abolish all discriminatory Laws and Acts laws against women and to introduce and adopt the bill regarding women's rights in accordance with CEDAW and directives of the Supreme Court, and

(c) to prepare ground for strong movement of women in the country.......

Appendix

Concrete Programs of All Nepal Women National Campaign 2000-2001

The tenure of ANWA will be for two years beginning in 13 April 2000. For the first year, it will run its programs in the half part of the country. The rest half of the country will be covered for the second year.

2. Each year, the total period of our Campaign of the year will be divided into four phases; (1) the first phase will include April, May and June, (2) the second phase will include July, August and September, (3) the third phase will include October, November and December and (4) the last phase will include January, February and March.

3. The following programs will be set for different time periods:

(a) The first phase (April, May and June): Press conference, publication of important and relevant documents, district level organization and reorganization of women's associations, expansion of organization at the initiatives of district committees, and collection of data on local level women's problems and initiatives to resolve these problems.

(b) The second phase (July, August and September): Initiation for organizational expansion, Campaign for membership, district level meetings, gatherings and conferences and discussion. During the meetings/gatherings or conferences, women workers will discuss about the preparation and deputation of local, district or national level women workers in their respective districts. fund-raising Campaign, training for women at local level.

(c) Third Phase (October, November and December): Final preparation of All Nepal Women's local and district level national Campaign programs in October, the local level Campaign in November and district level Campaign in December.

(d) Fourth Phase (January, February and March): Final preparation of All Nepal Women's National Campaign programs at national and district level in January, commencement of all Nepal Women's National Campaign from February

4. Effort will be made to mobilize all members and workers of

ANWA to a maximal level to launch All Nepal Women's National Campaign. At the same time, we should try to get maximum co-operation from other mass and friendly organization as well for the same cause.

5. VDC[15] Level Campaign: All Nepal Women's National Campaign will be held during mid November at VDC level. The Campaign will rui: for 15 days to a month. The date of commencement will be fixed by the district committee. The Campaign will be launched in each village and ward. If possible, various groups will be formed with the co-operation of district committee and other village level mass organizations for the Campaign. During VDC-level Campaign, effort should be made to fulfill the following activities:

(a) Distribution of membership, (b). Organization and re-organization of committees, (c) Sale distribution of literature on women, (d) Awareness programs for women about women's problems, (f) recruitment of women volunteers, (g) collection of donation, (6) preparation for and advocacy of district level Campaign and (h) Signature Campaign for women's demands.

6. District Level Campaign: During this Campaign, effort should be made to complete the VDC-level women's activities successfully and effectively. Analyzing the situation, this Campaign should cover almost all villages of the district. The programs should be well prepared prior to launch the Campaign.

7. The whole period of January should be devoted for the preparation of national Campaign. Attention should be paid to prepare (a) essential materials, such as pamphlets, banner, membership receipts, required for the Campaign, (b) essential materials, such as vehicles, required for the travel, (c) itinerary, rooms and boards, (d) final preparation of meetings and rally, (e) audio-video equipment and (f) enough fund for Campaign

8. We should try to accomplish various activities during national Campaign. These activities are (a) creation of broad-based public-opinion in favor of women's right and their demands, (b). propagation, sales and distribution of published materials on women, and (c) collection of signatures in favor of women's demands.

9. Depending upon situation, we should try to accomplish various programs in the district. These programs are (a) organization of mass-meeting and demonstration, (b) public relation and public dialogue, (c)

---

15. VDC stands for Village Development Committee. It is a local level administrative structure of the present day Nepal.

interaction programs in selected districts, d) meetings with women workers and activists, (e) distribution of membership, and (f) formation of district committees and meetings with them.

10. Concrete Fund-raising Programs: The concrete fund raising programs of ANWA are:

(a) Collection of fund for the Charter of Women's Rights National Campaign should start immediately after the national conference,

(b) Maximum fund collection should be made for the national Campaign during VDC and district level women's Campaign,

(c) Prior preparation should be made to organize Deusi/Bhailo[16] program for raising the fund.

(d) For October and November, concrete programs should be prepared for raising fund.

(e) During national Campaign, there should be one-day program at the towns enroute for raising funds.

(f) In every mass-meeting, a special fund raising program should be organized.

(g) We should raise our fund by selling cassettes, books, booklets and batches for women's national Campaign.

(h) We should make our maximum efforts to collect funds from industrialists, businessmen, intellectuals, human right activists and other institutions, friendly mass organizations, political parties and the Nepalese living abroad.

(i) We should try to find out other possible sources for fund raising, and

(j). We should open a separate saving account for women's national Campaign.

11. The Women's National Campaign should be accomplished within two years in the following ways:

(a) in the first year, we should launch our Campaign in Mahakali, Seti, Bheri, Rapti, Lumbini and Dhaulagiri zones, and

16. *Traditional cultural programs performed during Deepawali. Deepawali is an annual Hindu festival celebrated by lighting lamps and singing and dancing from door to door for raising funds.*

(b) in the second year, we should launch our Campaign in Mechi, Koshi, Sagarmatha, Janakpur, Narayani and Gandaki zones. There will be a month long separate program in Karnali by 2001. The first year final Campaign will be held in Kathmandu. In the second, the final Campaign will be help in Kathmandu only after completing various programs in different districts of Bagmati zone. Bagmati will be covered in the second year. The closing ceremony will be held in Kathmandu.

12. The following program should be held in Kathmandu.

(a) Presentation of a memorandum to the government with mass demonstration and collected signatures from various parts of Nepal.

(b) Demonstration and mass meeting in Kathmandu.

(c) Interaction and discussion about the problems of women.

13. Production of audio-video cassettes and batches and publication of pamphlets and posters.

14. Programs like organizational expansion, training for women, recruitment of women volunteers and fund raising should be organized in various districts of those zones which do not fall under the first year Campaign. Similar programs should be organized in other districts of those zones which do not fall under the second year Campaign.

15. We should make our efforts to win favor of other political parties, women's organizations and get support from them during to our national Campaign in various districts.

16. In order to succeed our Campaign, we should organize training program at different level in a systematic way.

Based on various suggestions from the districts, the central committee will have the right to change or revise the programs and give them a concrete shape.

Interrelationship between Charter of Women's Rights and Women's Liberation Movement

- Mohan Bikram Singh

(This paper on 'Interrelationship between Charter of Women's Rights and Women's Liberation Movement' was presented on April 23 2002 at a seminar organized by All Nepal Women's Association in course of the All Nepal Women's National Campaign 2002.)

(A)

Ladies and gentlemen,

First of all, let me extend my heartfelt welcome to all our distinguished guests as well as the valued participants in this seminar on 'Interrelationship between Charter of Women's Rights (CWR) and Women's Liberation Movement' for providing me this opportunity to present my views.

High importance is attached to the subject of the seminar since both CWR and 'International Women's Movement' parts of the topic are equally important and demand an in-depth and minute study. Here by CWR we mean the document adopted by All Nepal Women's Association (ANWA) in Butwal on March 1996. This CWR is based on the long and historical international women's liberation movement. Since it is also a link of the same, both of them are so closely related. I'd like to thank the organizers for organizing a seminar on such an important subject.

At the outset I'd like to shed some light on the role of the ANWA, generally, in the struggle of women's rights in Nepal and especially, in the preparation of CWR. I feel proud to tell you that ANWA has been playing

Comrade M.B. Singh is General Secretary of NCP (Mashal).

an important role in the movement of women for their rights. ANWA's history and related facts are enough to reveal how important role it has been playing in a planned way, generally for women's rights, and, especially, for the inheritance of the parental property which is significant in the Nepalese history.

As far as I know, all the materials related to it (ANWA's history) are going to be published in a book entitled 'Women's Liberation Movement Part I' scheduled to be released on April 14, 2002 in Kathmandu in the concluding ceremony of the Campaign.* Despite a remarkable role of ANWA in women's movement, media have always been indifferent towards it. Even the grand success of this Campaign which faced the challenges caused by emergency, deployment of army and activities of the Maoists has been either neglected or undermined by the Nepalese media. The Campaign which started from Kanchanpur on Feb. 28, 2002, has now arrived at Butwal with its success in the districts like Kailali, Bardia, Banke, Dang-Deukhuri, Pyuthan and Kapilvastu. From Butwal it will finally arrive in Kathmandu through Arghakhanchi, Palpa, Prvat, Myagdi and Baglung. Despite the persistent indifference of the media, facts are enough to reveal the glorious history of ANWA.

Actually, the present Campaign of ANWA was initiated in 1988. It was the time when ANWA's Second National Convention had been concluded at Gorakhpur in India. It was the high time of monarchy and Panchayati dictatorship. The Convention had passed 'Manifesto of ANW', which provided a theoretical base for the movement of the Association. The Extended Meeting of Central Committee of ANWA concluded at Butwal in 1991 passed a resolution for equal rights for son and daughters on property and raised the slogan: "Equal property to equal children". Immediately after a meeting, ANWA launched a demonstration which is first of its kind in the history of women's movement in Nepal organized for equal rights for daughter and son. The meeting also decided to organize seminars on 'Equal Property for Women' all over Nepal at village, district and central levels. Accordingly, the village level and district level seminars were held at first. The central level seminar was held in Kathmandu on 10 and 11 March1993. It was the first seminar ever held at three levels on a single subject in Nepal.

---

* The book was published under the title "महिला मुक्ति आन्दोलन, भाग-१" (Women's Liberation Movement, Part-1)

The first Extended Meeting of the Central Committee of ANWA held in Kushma village in Kapilvastu on Feb. 9, 1995 decided to launch Charter of Women's Rights National Campaign. In the theree stages of the Campaign, expansion of the organization, propaganda, press meets, district level women's gatherings, roundtable meetings, opinion collection, discussions on mass level, signature campaign, submission of memorandum at the parliament, demonstrations and mass meetings were held all over Nepal. At the fourth or final stage, the Central Committee Meeting of ANWA held in Butwal on March 22-23, 1996 passed 'CWR'. It also decided to celebrate April 10 as CWR Day every year. It is indeed a matter of pleasure that this seminar is being held at Butwal at the same day where CWR was adopted on half a decade before. The presence of our distinguished guests from Germany (Gabi and Thomos) has symbolically connected this seminar with international women's movement. The Fourth National Convention of ANWA held in April 7, 8 and 9, 2000, decided to launch a country-wide ANWA National Campaign in the first stage in west Nepal, then after in Eastern Nepal, Karnali and Bagmati Zone, says ANWA.

(B)

This CWR can also be called a historical document of the Nepalese women's movement. Women's Manifesto passed by the Second National Convention of ANWA and this Charter of Women's Rights throw light on the fundamental problems, principles, programmes and policies of women's liberation movement in Nepal

At the very beginning, CWR announces, 'Men and women are equal by birth'. Stressing on today's 'historical necessity' it says: 'Eliminating gender discrimination and semi-slavery, it is the historical need to provide them complete freedom and equality'. These two remarks are sufficient to make the basic nature and goal of the movement.

This section of the book also clarifies many other things of theoretical importance, which will be helpful to understand the fundamental problems and direction of the movement. This document holds the view that since women's liberation is an integral part of the liberation of all the working class people, it should not be treated in isolation. The present discriminatory and unequal state is the result of the complexwhole of the reactionary regime, economic and social system, laws, religion, culture, traditions, ethics, superstitions etc. Therefore, the CWR holds the view that for women's liberation, a prolonged and uncompromised struggle is a must.

The traditional view of the society strongly opposes women's just demands, however, it can neither minimise their importance nor can it check its success. In the past these people were against even Sati System (killing wives themselves by burning in the husband's funeral pyre), girls' education, widow marriage, love marriage by citing scriptures. But people's consciousness, women's movements as well as the changing process of society have weakened their stand. Likewise, the views against abortion, inheritance of parental property, divorce and remarriage are sure to be weakened. The CWR not only focuses on gender equality but also underlines the need of reservation and special facilities which are the prerequisites for equality. Provision of reservation is essential because of women's semi-slavery state of thousands of years. Besides, women's biology and reproduction also demand special provisions of permanent nature.

Globally and in Nepal also women's liberation movement has a long glorious and bright history. As a result of which several declarations, treaties, constitutional provisions, policies, laws have been adopted globally and in Nepal. UNO's Human Rights Declaration, General Agreement to End Discrimination Against Women, among others, are remarkable. All these are the result of the progressive, revolutionary and women's liberation movement of different countries at different times. However, they are not enough for complete freedom and equality. Moreover, even these provisions have not been implemented well. The CWR mentions that the UNO's treaties as well as the provisions of the constitution of Nepal have not been implemented in Nepal. Regarding the solution the CWR says : 'For women's freedom and equality much more work and struggle has to be done for the radical change of the reactionary system'.

The present form of family is also an obstacle to this end. In fact, family has been a jail for women. Today women are limited to the domestic sphere only. Regarding this, the CWR states : 'All religions, cultures, traditions and scriptures seek women to confine them within the four walls, and the effect of which can also be seen in the psychology of women. In fact, family reflects women's subordination and gender inequality much more than anything else.'

For the CWR radical change of the structure of family is 'decisive'. It further says, 'The present structure of family provides a foundation for the existing reactionary system.' Therefore, true liberation of women is not possible without destroying the existing structure of the family. And, for this, full participation of women, both in public sphere and in the field of production, which plays a decisive role for women's liberation. The CWR also draws our attention to the necessity of restructuring family on the foundation of new norms and values. Family should be the foundation for social development and true conjugal life. The CWR states; 'We can achieve the goal by restructuring family on the basis of freedom between men and women, equality, honour, true love and ideology.' The CWR opposes double standard on the questions of, ethics or conduct for men and women and emphasizes on the necessity of equal code of conduct for both for man and women.

The reactionary forces have always been opposing or the demands and movement of women for improvement in their condition. However, they can't check the process of change of the society because the material condition has a decisive role in it. It is the change in the material field that clears all the obstruction on the path. In turn, these changes also influence our consciousness, whereby, revolutionary consciousness and revolutionary movements are born, which again force the reactionary governments to declare reform of essential nature. As for example, the Sati System, slavery etc were abolished under the reactionary political systems. Likewise, women's situation is also improving. However the CWR states : 'Women's actual freedom, equality is impossible under the prevailing political system. It has to be radically changed. But for such a radical change, all the exploited, working class people and women have to move on unitedly.' The unity among them at international and national level can fundamentally solve the problem of all the exploited and women. Clarifying it, the CWR states; 'All the exploited, working class people and women are moving towards the same bright and revolutionary future.' Thus, the preamble of the CWR concludes; 'This CWR is a link of the same process of development.'

(C)

CWR, besides preamble, contains 9 chapters : equal property right to women, freedom of marriage and divorce, freedom of abortion, trafficking of women and prostitution, sexual harassment of women and violence, control over women's rights, security of minority, down-trodden women and the women of ethnic groups, family court and miscellaneous.

A great many questions such as equal wages to women workers, control of sexual harassment on them, exposure of the body of women in advertisement, problem of women employees, elimination of all the discriminatory laws against women, provision of reservation for women, among others have been raised in the Charter. Thus, it represents all the progressive movements going on in Nepal as well as in the world.

At different historical times, generally, the following women's issues are raised in the world :

1. Reduction of the working hours of women workers, increase in salary and improvement in the condition of work
2. Voting right
3. Freedom of marriage and divorce
4. Equal right to property
5. Freedom of abortion

Among them, voting right has been recognised globally and in Nepal. As for other demands, they have been addressed in different ways in different countries whereas in some countries they are yet to be fulfilled. In Nepal, we have to struggle hard for all the demands except voting right. His Majesty's Government has already signed the General Agreement on Women's Rights and the Elimination of All the Discriminations against Them. But in practice, many discriminatory laws, discrimination in family and in public sphere and oppression against them still persist. In fact, the Nepalese women are still facing the medieval condition, and some of the improvements of bourgeoisie nature which have been old in other countries are yet to be fulfilled through struggles. The CWR presents all the demands of Nepalese women very clearly. Therefore, we can hope that it will provide a fundamental theoretical base for women's movement in Nepal for a long time to come.

Among the women's demands, the demand of equal property right is of high importance. The root cause of women's subordination is their economic dependence on men. History teaches us a class economically weak and dependent is bound to be politically and socially also weak. Therefore, the root cause of women's inequality can be found in their economic condition. The CWR states : 'Women's equality and freedom is not possible without their economic equality and freedom. Hence, equal property right is decisive and fundamental for gender equality.'

The question 'whether women should have right over parental property or the property of husband is nonsense. There should not be any condition or limitation. In fact, women must inherit parental property, and, after marriage, both husband and wife must have equal right over the property. Such a right should be recognized as an inborn right. Women should not be denied such a right in case of their crime or punishment also. In this connection, the CWR states : 'To ensure this right, there should not be any condition like divorce, remarriage, remarriage without formal divorce, illicit sexual relation. among others.' In fact, in the earning of property, management of it, its growth and safety, women play an equal role and sometimes even more important role than male. Therefore, property right is neither mercy nor grace but in fact, they deserve it.

The condition under which men don't lose their property, women have to lose. It can't be just. Recently the parliament has made a law under which women have to return their parental property after their marriage, which is discriminatory because men don't have to do so after their marriage. Such a discriminatory provision is patriarchal, and can, in no way, be called just.

The CWR analysing the freedom of marriage, divorce, abortion presents the objective demands concerning them. Regarding divorce, the CWR states 'We must have the right either to live alone with property or remarry or divorce if we are oppressed or tortured in the family or are denounced, abused by the husbands or if husbands remarry or the thread of conjugal life is broken between husband and wife. Even after divorce or remarriage, the right over the property must be retained.' Previously totally banned, the recent bill passed by the parliament has partially recognized the freedom of divorce. This is also the partial success of the movement.

However, much has yet to be done for full freedom. To cite an example, in India, an unmarried girl can abort if she wishes but in Nepal such provision has not been made. Regarding abortion right the CWR states; 'There should not be any condition in abortion except for the adverse effect on the life of the concerned woman.'

(D)

The demands of the CWR are in line of the progressive and just demands of international women's liberation movement and also the movement of Nepal. It is the tradition of international women's movement to put forth inclusive demands so as to further the struggle for women's liberation.

In course of the struggle against feudalism and for capitalistic democracy, the exploited and oppressed classes of people and other sections of people became conscious of their freedom, liberation and organisation. Women were not exception to it. During the period of Renaissance in Europe, women showed their dissatisfaction over the traditional feudal restrictions, norms and values and took initiative for their liberation. With the completion of industrial revolution and the emerging wave of capitalistic revolution women came up with concrete demands for their liberation and also began to be organised. Confined within the four walls in the age of feudalism, capitalism brought them out into the market and they started working in industries. Thus, capitalism opened up public sphere for them from their confinement within the four wall.

The Bourgeois democratic revolution against feudalism had its impact not only on economy and politics but also on philosophy, culturel and ideology. Along with other exploited and oppressed classes of people, women became conscious of struggle casting away traditional and backward thinking. With the gradual downward movement of feudalistic economy and the gradual rise of bourgeois democratic movement, women previously confined within the four walls, have began to come out in the public sphere and have started working in industries, professions and NGOs and INGOs. The process of change over the past fifty years makes the point clear. These changes in economic and social fields have changed the conservative and traditional thinking of women, which in turn, inspired women to struggle for their liberation.

The American and the French revolutions have made a big contribution to the world revolutionary movements. During the American Revolution (1775-83) there was a strong demand to make constitutional provisions regarding women's issues. During the French Revolution also (1789) there had been the 'Declaration of Men's and Women Citizen's Rights'. Accordingly, Olympe de Gouges had presented 'The Declaration of the Rights of Women' in the national assembly. Not only this, it was during the French Revolution that women had formed 'Revolutionary Women's Club', which was the first women's organisation in the world. In 1884, at New York in America, the first Congress of Citizen's Rights was organised, which had issued a manifesto for women's legal freedom, complete educational and professional opportunity and voting rights. In this connection, mention should also be made of the book 'A Vindication of the Rights of Women' which draws the outline of the feminist movement of the nineteenth century.

In the history of women's liberation movement, they struggled for the increase of salary, reduction of working hours and against the inhuman management of the factories. It was on March 8 that the women working in garments and cloth mills went on strikes and demonstrated in New York for these demands. In the history of Women's Liberation Movement, the struggle for voting right is also remarkable. Today, women all over the world are using this right which was the achievement of a long and very hard struggle. In Japan, Italy, U.S.A., Germany, France and Switzerland women got the right 20, 26, 50, 51, 96 and 123 years after men, respectively. Such a conservative point of view of the so-called leading, democratic and developed countries shown towards women's issue is deplorable. Legally, this right has been granted in almost every country. At least, this right can't be a demand anywhere. Despite that, as long as there remains patriarchal subordination, domination and oppression, even the voting right of women will be controlled by men.

In principle, most of the countries have accepted women's property right. Even the UNO declaration and the General Agreement on the

Elimination of Women have also recognised it. Despite it when that comes to implementing them, many limitations and conditions are imposed. As a result, this right of women is not translated into practice. Gabi, a German woman leader who is present here as our distinguished guest as well as the letters from some German women to the Nepalese women tell us that Germany has granted equal property right to women. However in practice, this right can't be fully used by woman. Therefore, in reality, women's property right in Germany is unequal.

The freedom of abortion has not even recognised by the UNO owing to the strong opposition on the part of the orthodox Muslims. However, world opinion is very strong for it. As a result, traditionalists' view of complete restriction on abortion has been weakened and most of the countries of the world have loosened their restrictions on abortion.

Women have also been struggling hard globally against violent, physical and mental torture in family and in the society. As a result of which, such misbehaves and crimes against women have been made illegal. But, in practice, especially in the villages of the third world countries, women become victims of such behaves and crimes. Worst of all, no legal action is taken against such misdeeds. In fact, women have to go through a long and hard struggle against all these issues. As a result of it, it is clear; women have to go through a hard and large struggle on almost except at subject the voting right.

Whatever rights women have got so far are the result of different kinds of struggles as well as the development in physical and technical fields. The world women's liberation movement has definitely played an important role on it. Besides, revolutionary movements contributed a lot to the improvement of women's condition as well as to make women's liberation movement more effective. Besides, the impact of European Renaissance, Industrial Revolution, development of revolutionary theories and the capitalist and socialist revolutions of different countries can't be minimized.

The impact of American Revolution, French Revolution, Russian Socialist Revolution on women's liberation movement is self evident. Especially, Marxism-Leninism and socialist movements have helped women's liberation movement a lot. Marxism-Leninism and socialism attach much importance to liberating all the working class people from all kinds of exploitation and subordinations. And, not less importance is attached to the liberation of women, being an integral part of the total liberation movement. Thus, what is self-evident is the decisive role played by Marxism-Leninism and socialist movements in the liberation movement of women. On the whole, we can say that as an inseparable part of the total liberation movement, women's liberation movement will go on and on. And, finally, women will also be liberated along with exploited and oppressed working class people.

(E)

We can say that women's liberation movement began with French Revolution (1789) with the preparation of 'The Manifesto of Women's Rights'. It was then that revolutionary women were organised. The Manifesto begins : 'By nature women are free and equal to men in all rights'. In a period of over two hundred years, the liberation movement of women has been able to get equal rights to a large extent. However, women's liberation movement has to go a long way to end all kinds of exploitations, oppression, subordination and discrimination. International women's liberation movement has also contributed a lot to whatever rights women have got in Nepal. As for example, Jung Bahadur was forced to abolish Sati System in Nepal only because of the international liberation movement as there was no movement in Nepal against it. A long list of such examples can be given. Nepal owes to the international revolution movements for the development of liberation movement and improvement in the condition of women. Along with Marxist-Leninist theories, socialist revolution and international communist movement, the declaration and treaties of the UN have had a remarkable effect. These are only a few examples to clarify the impact of international women's liberation movement on the movement of Nepal.

Today, the demands of equal right to parental property, freedom of marriage and divorce, abortion, elimination of discriminatory codes of conduct, end of violence and oppression and establishment of family court put forth by ANWA, are facing a serious opposition. But it is not a new thing viewing in the history of world women's liberation movement. Whatever the opposition, the glorious movement of women will not be ended. What can be said undoubtedly is that facing all the obstacles and challenges, women's liberation movement in Nepal will go on achieving more and more heights.

During the French Revolution, 'The Manifesto of Men and Women Citizen's Rights' was rejected by the national parliament. The bourgeois rulers who took over after the revolution, not only rejected the manifesto but also gave capital punishment to Olempe de Gauges who prepared the manifesto. Not only this, they also crushed the first women's club in the history of women's movement. In New York on March 8, 1847 garment women gathered demanding the reduction of working hours, increase of salary and the improvement of the work place, were severely beaten up by the police and their struggle was crushed. But they could not crush woman's movement forever. On the contrary, March 8 became the international women labourers' day, which was something beyond imagination for the rulers who crushed the struggle of March 8, 1847. Even voting right for women was strongly opposed, but today it has been recognised all over the world. In England in 1838 Chartists had included the voting right for women, but later it was removed.

In Iran in 1911 ruling out the voting rights for women the Islamic leaders had said, 'we shouldn't think over the issue simply because it is against the code of conduct of the Islamic parliament because God has not bestowed necessary abilities upon them to take part in politics'. In Japan in 1928, the then home minister told the women demanding voting right : 'Go home and wash your children's cloths because you deserve it.'

Not only reactionary, orthodox and bourgeois forces but also those who call themselves socialists also are found to hold such views. In Germany in 1875, August Bebel's proposal of women's voting right was rejected by the Conference of the Socialist Democratic Party.

We can cite a great many such examples in this respect. In Germany in 1863, the German Workers' Association formed under the leadership of Lasalle proposed against allowing women to work in factory s well as not issuing them the membership of trade union. Behind this point of view was working the traditional and conservative attitude that women are weak and that they deserve work only in the domestic sphere. In the first Convention of International Labourers' Association, where Marx and Engels also were present, there was a hot debate on whether women should be allowed to work in factores or not. Especially, the French anarchists came up with the view that women deserve domestic sphere. Working in factories is physically, morally and socially also harmful for them. Needless to say, Marx and Engels struggled hard against such views. They were of the opinion that women's participation in the mode of production prepares foundation for their liberation movement. However, opinion was rejected as the labourers' movement then was in the grip of traditionalists and petty-bourgeoisie. But later, the participation of women went on increasing with the weakening of conservative ideas among the workers.

The conservative and petty bourgeois views against which the Europeans struggled some hundred and fifty years age, we have to do the same in Nepal today. All the feudal, reactionary, conservative and petty bourgeois forces are against the progressive demands of women stressing that they deserve being confined within the depressing, dark and narrow domestic sphere away from the light of the public sphere, where there is prestige, optimism and a chance of self actualisation. So much so that even the so-called Marxist-Leninist and progressives organisation have not been able to do away with such views.

The question is not limited only to it. In Nepal, not only among the reactionary or conservative forces but also among the so-called Marxist-Leninists, we find the effect of such conservative and non-Marxist-Leninist views towards women's liberation movement as well as women's just demands. In this context, what is mentionable is the example of Nepal Peasants' and Labourers' Party. It has been consistently opposing the demand of women's equal property right. It was due to this stance of this party that nine or ten left parties have not been unanimous to approve the demand of women's equal property rights. What is also mentionable here is that, the party has been opposing the demand of land ceiling. These events can be compared with the Social Democratic Parties' Conference in Germany in 1875 which had opposed the demand of voting right for women. In this connection, I would like to state some of the conservative and non-revolutionary point of view of Communist Party of Nepal (Mashal) also. The Political report adopted by the Sixth Party Congress held in 2051 is enough to shed light on it.

The Report describing the prevailing 'conservative' point of view in the Party states : 'Still we find the presence of conservative point of view in the Party.... to a large extend especially regarding untouchability, family, women, property, sex, marriage, divarce and religious rituals ... we are more guided and influenced by the backward thinking.' Regarding such weaknerses or the party cadres the Report states : 'There is a narrow and conservative view point working in the party towards women to a large degree.... . Even the party members are conservative on the issue... . What is more serious is the suspicious and narrow view regarding the character of women. And, worst of all, they are evaluated more not on the basis of their role in theoretical, political or organizational activities but on the basis of trivial personal matters. What can be said comfortably is the dual standard is adopted form men and women carders while considering on their character and morality.'

What will be the result of such a conservative perspective? Regarding it the Report states: 'Not only on political issue, but also on social issues, our Party should adopt revolutionary outlook and play a leading role in social transformation. But such a conservative outlook prevailing in the party has checked us to play such a role and has left us behind.

Needless to interpret further, such a conservative and backward outlook prevailing in the party is the reflection of such thinking deeply rooted in our feudal, conservative, patriarchal and backward society. The objection of the Social Democratic Conference held in Germany to the bill of voting right of women, the proposal on limiting women to the domestic sphere in the first International and the stance of Nepal Peasants' and workers' Party against the equal property right are some of the examples before us. So, it is not surprising if our party also has such weaknesses. But what is remarkable is that such view has weakened our party to play a leading role in the transformation of the society. Therefore, following the examples of Marx, Engels, who had struggled hard against such

(167)

conservative views, the Report has rightly emphasised on the necessity of struggle against such weakness of the party.

What is clear from the above description is that the stance against women's liberation movement and women's just demands is nothing new in the world. What is also evident is that such an opposition will not stop the liberation movement of women. There is sufficient ground to claim with the passage ᴄ ime women's demands will gradually but definitely be fulfilled and thosє ho are against their movement as well as their just demands are bound to be defeated. We are sure that the demands mentioned in the CWR be fulfilled in the end.

Finally, we'd like to clarify that the CWR is an unseparable part of the world women's liberation movement. What should also be taken into consideration is that for the true liberation of women, the liberation movement has to gain new heights. And, with the unity of all the exploited, oppressed working class people as well as the revolutionary forces, the liberation will definitely be a success.

Appendix-F

Comment on the Paper presented in the Seminar

— Gabriele Beisenkamp

(Comment made on the paper "The Interrelationship between the Charter of Women's Right and the International Women's"in the seminar held at Butwal on April 23, 2002)

Dear Friends,

I will thank you very much to ANWA for the invitation to this Campaign. This is an very important step for the <u>fraternal relation or</u> of the women's movement from Nepal and Germany. And we make the experience, that the women of both countries are very interested about the different life conditions and the struggle for liberation.

Now let me speak about the Charta of Women's Right.

This Charta is an important step for the struggle for equal right's of women in Nepal. And I agree with this Charta.

I agree with your demands for equal property rights for the women and also the right of marriage and divorce. I was very surprised that at the meetings and also at the press conferences, some men had the opinion that the property right or the right to divorce will destroy your social system. I have to this men a other question. Had a social system the right to exist, that destroy the life of half of his people?

In Germany we have the property right and also the right of divorce since a long time. And since 1970 the equal rights are completely introduced. And I can tell you not the equal right destroy the social system. This social system destroy more and more the life of the people, because the only thing, what is really important for those who are in power is the profit of the monopoly.

To have the equal right is a very important step for the women's liberation. Because you need the democratic rights, to develop your self and take part at the social life. And also to struggle for the liberation.

But also Lenin told us.

"Notwithstanding all the laws emancipating women, she continues to be a domestic slave.....The real emancipation of women, real communism, will begin only where and when an all-out struggle begins against this petty housekeeping, or rather when its wholesale transformation into a large-scale socialist economy begins."

So with the equal rights our struggle for liberation has reached a important goal but the struggle will go on.

That the hole developing of the human being is a private task of the family, this is the reason, why in spite of the equal rights in our country the social inequality became more and more evidently. We had to chance the economic system but also the bourgeoisie family system, which manifests all work at home in the responsibility of the women. This bourgeoisie family systems is also the reason for the special exploitation an oppression of the women in our society.

In your Charta you speak about the family structure, which you want to prove. I agree with this. This is an very important task you formulated in your Charta.

Because when I speak here in Nepal with the women after the meetings, I noticed similar problems. Not only the so called women's issues are important for them, they are angry about their daily life circumstances. (Where to get water, grass for the buffalos, why had the husbands to work in foreign countries, and so on.)

It is the opinion of our party that it is a decide task, for the ML parties and the women's movement to struggle against this life circumstance the broad masses are forced to live. And also become knowledge's about the oppressive function of this family system.

I read from the book: Class struggle and the struggle for the liberation of women:

"The intensification of the general crisis of capitalism increasingly jeopardizes the masses' conditions of life worldwide.... A worldwide tendency to absolute pauperization of the masses becomes apparent.

(170)

The biggest burden is borne by the masses of women, because they have to maintain the conditions of life often under the most difficult circumstances.

Traditional forms of life and family structures such as village communities and extended families are destroyed. But bourgeois and petty-bourgeois family relations hardly can be realized by the bulk of the world population. Imperialism thus engenders a *worldwide absence of family among the masses* in conjunction with mass unemployment and underemployment, rural exodus, life in slums, migrant work, refugee movements and wars.....

The result of this destruction of the foundations of life of hundreds of millions of people is that women increasingly come into contradiction with imperialism. The *international women's movement began its rise* precisely in response to this development. As women increasingly recognize imperialist exploitation and oppression as the root cause of their situation, their *struggle for women's liberation acquires an anti-imperialist character.* It thus becomes a part of the worldwide struggle for liberation from imperialism."

I think it is an very important step to discuss with the broad masses of women, that it is the imperialistic system, which destroy their life and their families. So it will be possible that the women's movement become an anti-imperialist character, and will be an part of the worldwide struggle for liberation from imperialism.

I also agree with your demands against women traffic and prostitution, and also against violence against women.

We know all this problems too. In Germany we have about 400.000 prostitutions. And our Government actually discuss a law which makes the prostitution to a normal profession. So they will legalise the sexual oppression of the women.

We have also demands in our party program against this.

Like: Punishment of sexual exploitation and violence!

Banning and prosecution of violent and child pornography.

But we know also that the prostitution can not be abolished in an exploiting system. Lenin told that prostitution can be abolished only when we have abolished the capitalistic society. So long people be forced to sell there labour power prostitution will be exist.

(171)

Also this knowledge's we shall discuss.

Your wrote about the UN Declaration of women's rights in the Charta of women's right. This declaration was an important step. But I think, it is necessary, to observe the developing of the UN work. Because the UN is also an instrument of imperialism. I read again in the book "The class struggle and the struggle for liberation of women". Page 171

" In their struggle for equality, for an time the women of the world apparently received support form the official policy of the United Nations and the World Bank, and even got funds."

They make this because the system of neo-colonialism is dependent upon the political and social participation of women, which calls for at least a minimum of formal legal and social equality. This was the background of the UN efforts toward equality for men and women, which began in 1975.

"Since the imperialist-dominated UN has no interest in the development of a militant women's movement, *petty-bourgeois feminism* was systematically injected into the international women's movement through the UN and especially so-called nongovernmental organizations (NGOs), and has become an *element of neocolonialist rule.*

An important effect of the women's policy of these NGOs is the division between men and women and between women's movement and revolutionary movement." (S.172)

"You also have al lot experience with this kind of NRO policy launched by the imperialistic states. I think it is very important that the women recognize this petty-bourgeois feminism and are able to stand up to the corrosive influence of the petty-bourgeois mode of thinking.

The last topic I want to speak is how to organise the international movement. The visit of Durga Paudel last year in Germany and now our visit in Nepal are very important steps to develop this international women's movement. And you can be sure, that I make a lot of lessens in Germany about this campaign, so that the women's movement in Germany becomes an international alignment.

But first I will say that I am very happy to see, that your campaign and the Charta of Women's right has big agreement by other organisations and women of other parties. Also a member of the ruling party National Congress congratulate Durga Paudel for her speak.

(172)

That is possible because the oppression don't stop for the classes. In the *responsibility of women for private housekeeping and family affairs management* lies the material foundation for the double oppression of the masses of women in capitalism.

So it is possible that in the militant women's movement are women from the different classes. This will be able, only when the organization works at überparteilichen foundation. **(not party-affiliated)** We developed some principles on which basis it is possible to work together with people with different world-outlooks. I want to introduce some of this principles, because they are very important to develop the militant women's movement also on an international level. The following principles have proved successful:

- Unity on the basis of equality and struggle

- Close linkage with the working-class movement

- Realize a culture of debate in an atmosphere of objectivity and solidarity

- International solidarity

- Openness to a social perspective of a society freed from exploitation of man by man

- Equal participation of Marxist-Leninists." (pp. 81-82)

In 1996 the Germen women's league Courage developed a suggestion to an network platform for the international networking of the women's movement. I will introduce this to you.

After the description of the world wide. situation there were formulated the following goals: I quote:

Goals

1. Our vision for an international network is a life in independency, freed from oppression and exploitation, in harmony with our natural surrounding, in peace and nations-friendship with the possibilities of equal rights in job, education, family and participation at political, cultural and social life. But this is incompatible with the ruling world economic system. Therefore we are looking for an alternative social system.

2. It is necessary to sensitize women all over the world to understand and to change economical and political connections. Together with the

youth we need to work out demands which can internationally join together millions of people.

Strategies

1. Building up a strong, militant political anti-imperialist women's movement. In Germany we therefore work closely together with other women's organizations.

2. Alliance with other political and social movements on a national and international scale: women-, female- and male-workers-, liberation-, youth-, environment~ and peace-movements.

3. International networking of basic movements is based on mutual support and mutual learning and is no one-way road.

4. It comes to reality by means of uncensored exchange of information and opinion. To learn about the particular situation of the countries and about the position of the women there for mutual understanding, accepting and tolerating their history and their developed culture. Carrying out internationally coordinated actions and activities like clearing up campaigns, signature collections, solidarity declarations, protests, demonstrations, strikes, house- and land-occupations. Therefore we need to take use of being present in the mass media.

5. The power for a change lies in a thorough basic work. We address to women who take their interests in their own hands. We can not give away our interests and activities to female lobbyists and female experts who are acting as our representatives. But lobby and parliamentary work can be useful as a speaking tool."

At the end they formulate also some principles like them I had introduced to you. I think on this network platform it will be possible to make the international women's movement inseparable and give her an anti-imperialistic orientation.

Danebad !